MEMORIES

OF EUROPE'S FUTURE

Significant Issues Series
Timely books presenting current CSIS research and analysis of interest to the academic, business, government, and policy communities.
Managing editor: Roberta L. Howard

≈   ≈   ≈

The Center for Strategic and International Studies (CSIS), established in 1962, is a private, tax-exempt institution focusing on international public policy issues. Its research is nonpartisan and nonproprietary.

CSIS is dedicated to policy analysis and impact. It seeks to inform and shape selected policy decisions in government and the private sector to meet the increasingly complex and difficult global challenges that leaders will confront in the next century. It achieves this mission in three ways: by generating strategic analysis that is anticipatory and interdisciplinary; by convening policymakers and other influential parties to assess key issues; and by building structures for policy action.

CSIS does not take specific public policy positions. Accordingly, all views, positions, and conclusions expressed in this publication should be understood to be solely those of the author.

The CSIS Press
Center for Strategic and International Studies
1800 K Street, NW
Washington, DC 20006
Telephone: (202) 887-0200
Fax: (202) 775-3199
E-mail: books@csis.org
Web site: http://www.csis.org/

MEMORIES
OF EUROPE'S FUTURE

FAREWELL TO YESTERYEAR

SIMON SERFATY

FOREWORD BY ROBERT B. ZOELLICK

THE CSIS PRESS

**Center for Strategic
and International Studies**
Washington, D.C.

Chapter 2 Adapted with permission from Simon Serfaty, *Stay the Course: European Unity and Transatlantic Solidarity* (Westport, Conn.: Praeger, an imprint of Greenwood Publishing Group, Inc., 1997), pp. 1–6 and 37–50. Sections of this chapter were presented at the Cooperation Project of the TransAtlantic Policy Network, Spring Meeting, Paris, France, April 1998. A similar argument was published in "Anos de Europa, Tiempo de cambios, Un caso de continuidad," *Meridiano Ceri*, no. 18 (December 1997), pp. 4–7.

Chapter 3 Adapted with permission from "Security Challenges in Europe after NATO Enlargement," in Stephen Blank, ed., *Security Challenges in Europe after NATO Enlargement: New Challenges, New Missions, New Forces* (Carlisle, Penn.: Army War College, September 1998), pp. 57–72. A short section of this chapter is adapted from "Europe and its Union," *Jobs & Capital* 7, no. 1 (Winter 1998), pp. 80–83.

Chapter 4 Sections of this chapter are adapted from "Expansion de l'OTAN et de l'Union Européenne," *Forum du Futur* (Winter 1997/98), pp. 37–40, and "Europa e Nato: Destini incrociati," *LiMes*, no. 1 (1998), pp. 291–296. An early version of this essay was prepared for *The National Debates Over the Ratification of NATO Enlargement*, CSIS Report, ed. Simon Serfaty and Stephen Cambone (Washington, D.C.: Center for Strategic and International Studies, October 1997).

Chapter 5 Adapted, with permission and deletion of some notes, from "Algeria Unhinged: What Next? Who Cares? Who Leads?" *Survival* 38, no. 4 (Winter 1996/97), pp. 137–153, by permission of Oxford University Press.

Chapter 6 Reprinted with permission, minor revisions, and deletion of some notes from "Bridging the Gulf across the Atlantic: Europe and the United States in the Persian Gulf," *Middle East Journal* 52, no. 3 (Summer 1998), pp. 337–350.

Chapter 7 Adapted with permission, minor revisions, and deletion of some notes from "Memories of Leadership," *Brown Journal of World Affairs* 5, no. 2 (Summer/Fall 1998), pp. 3–16. A short additional section is adapted from "A Certain Air of Destiny: To Win the Peace," *International Politics* 35, no. 4 (December 1998), pp. 450–460.

The CSIS Press, Washington, D.C. 20006
Printed on recycled paper in the United States of America
02 01 00 99   4 3 2 1

ISSN 0736-7136
ISBN 0-89206-347-5

Library of Congress Cataloging-in-Publication Data

Memories of Europe's future: Farewell to yesteryear / Simon Serfaty. Foreword by Robert B. Zoellick.   (Significant issues series, v. 21, no. 1)
    Includes bibliographical references and index.
    ISBN 0-89206-347-5
        1. Europe—Politics and government—20th century. 2. Europe—Foreign relations —United States. 3. United States—Foreign relations—Europe. I. Title. II. Series.
D443.S458   1999   98-43731
940.56—dc21   CIP

Contents

Foreword   vii

Introduction   **1**

PART ONE: Half Past NATO   **9**

1
Farewell to Yesteryear   **11**

2
Years of Europe   **16**
Why Care? 16   What Next? 20   Who Leads? 27

3
Steadfast and Changing   **30**
The Empires Come Home 33   America Comes Home 39
Common Home 43

PART TWO: Half Past NATO,
Half Before Europe   **45**

4
The Logic of Dual Enlargement   **47**
The Acquis Is the Key 53   Dual Enlargement 57
Old World Renewed 66

v

PART THREE: Half Before Europe   77

5
Bridging the Gap in the Mediterranean   79

Algeria Unhinged 81   Which War, Whose Crisis? 86
No Will to Lead 92

6
Bridging the Gulf across the Atlantic   105

Europe's Interests in the Persian Gulf 106   The Limits of Dual
Containment 111   Dialogue and Containment 117

7
Memories of Leadership   124

The Way to Lead 124   No Will to Follow 127
A Certain Air of Destiny 135

Index   143
About the Author   149

Foreword

A CENTURY AGO, IN 1899, Europe was in a hopeful mood. In that year, at the invitation of Czar Nicholas II, the countries of Europe met at The Hague with the United States to consider disarmament, limits on methods of warfare, and the creation of a permanent court to arbitrate international disputes. In France, Britain, and Germany, revisionist Socialists were exploring whether they could pursue their goals for society by working as members of national governments, thereby launching the great Social Democratic political parties of Europe. While the industrial revolution had come at a high price, the nations and peoples of Europe seemed to be searching for ways to channel their energy into the engines of a new, civilized age.

The dynamic United States was being drawn back to the affairs of the Old World in 1899. Having quickly dispatched Spanish fleets in the Caribbean and the Pacific, the United States was debating its larger role in the world. Foreign capital, especially from England, was helping to finance America's incredible economic growth, although the Americans suffered recurring panics when the banking policies of the day drew gold back to European vaults. Nevertheless, the U.S. capitalists profited enough to be able to send young, wealthy heiresses to titled but threadbare suitors in Britain, even to a family named Churchill.

In return, Europeans sent large numbers of less well-heeled and less well-known families to America's shores in the 1890s, including my own. This great movement of people gave the United States and Europe a common heritage at the same time that it contributed to different national conceptions.

While these events, large and small, were taking place, while hopes were growing for the promise of a new century, Europe was edging toward a precipice. That next century—the twentieth—

would prove to be Europe's most devastating. The Continent devoured itself, not once, but twice within 50 years. In the second half of the century, these calamities left Europe's fortune in the hands of two powers from the periphery of Europe—the Soviet Union and the United States.

Ten years ago, the defining politics of the twentieth century drew to a close with surprising rapidity, fortunately peacefully. The collapse of the Soviet Union created an opening for Russia to chart a new and nonimperial future. The end of the division of Germany and of Europe offered a real opportunity to reunite the Continent, to fulfill the best dreams of 1899.

How will Europe write the story of the next century? This is the question that Simon Serfaty takes up in this fine series of essays.

Dr. Serfaty knows that America's special relationship with Europe did not begin with the Cold War, nor will it end with that epic era. Europe and North America are linked by ties of culture, religion, business, institutions, and shared experience. But they also must contend with some European fears of disproportionate American influence, and some American suspicions of European intrigues.

As Europe and the United States consider their prospects in the next century, they would be mistaken, as Dr. Serfaty explains, to rely just on old habits. Europeans and Americans need to think through all their interests, not just at home and across the Atlantic, but also in the wider world. They need to assess the values for which they will strive. And they need to decide whether and how to adapt their institutions of cooperation. In particular, they need to consider the future course of the two great institutional creations of the second half of the century, the European Union and NATO.

Europe already is a global economic power. The introduction of the euro will enhance its influence further. Now Europe must decide how it will use that strength.

In contrast, Europe's military weight is modest, although it could play a far greater role. Given the dangers the democracies will face in the next century, I hope Europe will recognize its potential to benefit common values and interests.

Perhaps the primary lesson of 1899 is to be humble about our ability to forecast the future. But another lesson may be that the actions of leaders, the ideas of thinkers, and the decisions of publics matter a great deal to the course of history. I hope that this book will contribute to better decisions for the era we are entering.

Robert B. Zoellick
President, CSIS

Introduction

THIS VOLUME GATHERS ESSAYS that were written, for the most part, over an 18-month period in 1997–1998 and published in various forms on both sides of the Atlantic. They are about Europe and the ever closer Union that 15 nation-states have formed to bid farewell to their common history of division and conflict. They are also, directly or by implication, about these states' relations with the United States, which effectively saved the Europeans from their worst instincts during and after each of the three global wars waged in the twentieth century. Finally, the essays that follow are about Europe's relations with, and transatlantic relations over, the countries south of the Mediterranean—a region that the states of Europe used to rule before they bid farewell to their imperial history.

My intention was to reproduce these essays as they were written originally. Upon reviewing them, however, it became apparent that they would have to be slightly adapted individually before they could be presented collectively. These minor revisions (additions or deletions) were made primarily to account for developing events, whether predictable or not; to avoid repetitive statements from one essay to the next; or, even more fundamentally, to lighten the style—with fewer references to sources, for example. The revisions were not designed to transform the original argument, change the terms of the initial analysis, or redirect the early conclusions. In any case, hardly enough time has elapsed since each essay was first written to gain the new hindsight from which new wisdom reportedly grows.

These papers are grouped in three different clusters organized around the clock of transatlantic relations as "half past NATO" and "half before Europe"—"half past NATO" when celebrating

Europe's ability to sustain, after the Cold War, an historic transformation that began during the Cold War under the protective tutelage of the North Atlantic Treaty Organization; "half before Europe" when recognizing NATO's primacy as the U.S. institution of choice to address security issues in and on behalf of Europe; and "half before Europe, half past NATO" when pointing to the limits of either institution to cater alone to the satisfaction of interests, mainly outside the European continent, that are shared in common even when they are not shared evenly.

The three essays that form the first cluster all address, in different ways, the same question: Does Europe matter? Chapter 1 was written in mid-1997 as a mood piece for a project involving the Philip Morris Foundation. The short answer it proposes is based on Europe's remarkable capacity for self-renewal and the boldness shown by its nation-states to reverse the course of their shared history. However unrepeatable the post-1945 experience of Europe may be in other regions that remain fragmented and belligerent, it may be the inspiration for the worthy goals of reconciliation and integration elsewhere. Chapter 2 addresses the question of Europe's relevance, more specifically, to the United States. Admittedly, U.S. interests in Europe, however defined, are not likely to change from one year to the next, and this chapter repeats, therefore, themes I had developed in other writing, including a previous book, *Stay the Course*, written in early 1997. Such repetition is intentional. The reality of U.S. interests is too deep, and the scope of these interests too wide, not to deserve mention at every opportunity. Finally, Chapter 3 was initially drafted as an opening address for a conference organized by the Strategic Studies Institute (SSI) of the U.S. Army War College in late January 1998. It discusses Europe's evolution—steadfast and changing—during the Cold War relative to its prewar history: the death of empires, the birth of centrist republics, the end of total war, America's return, and the erosion of national sovereignty.

Chapter 4 stands alone in the second cluster of essays because the logic of dual enlargement that it seeks to formulate depends on the complementarity of both the European Union (at half past NATO) and NATO (at half before the EU). Whether with regard to the past or in anticipation of the future, neither institution can be discussed without some appreciation of what the other does and how it operates. With regard to the question of enlargement, the EU and NATO weave a pattern of complementary and even converging parallelism whereby what is started separately can be completed jointly because only together can these two institutions satisfy all needs of their members and partners, security as well as political, economic as well as societal. Hence the attempt to suggest a formula that would aim at achieving progressively an overlapping European membership for both NATO and the EU, while avoiding the neglect of institutional orphans that would belong to neither.

The first two essays included in the final cluster cross the Mediterranean and enter the Greater Middle East—Algeria in the Maghreb region, Iran and Iraq in the Persian Gulf. There, the time is neither that of Europe nor of NATO, but of both because neither institution (and none of their respective members) can lead alone, and neither (because of separate though not separable interests) can remain indifferent to the policies and attitudes of the other. The Algerian crisis examined in Chapter 5 is fairly typical of the instabilities that have characterized the post–Cold War years: a crisis that raises traditional economic and security issues together with cultural, religious, and ethnic questions, but also a crisis that Western countries can do little to alleviate notwithstanding its importance and that of the region it affects. The chapter was first drafted in the summer of 1996 as a paper for the Institute of National Strategic Studies at the National Defense University in Washington, D.C., was revised for publication in the London-based journal *Survival* the following winter, and was revised anew before its inclusion in this volume. Chapter 6 develops comparable themes of transatlantic discord and cooperation in the Persian Gulf. It was first drafted for an international conference organized by the Nixon Center at the Wye River Center in May 1997, many months before finding its way, with minor revisions, into the *Middle East Journal* in the summer of 1998.

Finally, the volume ends with a few "memories of leadership" that I evoked for an essay written in the spring of 1998 for Brown University's *Journal of World Affairs*. Woven into this piece is a short section adapted from an essay review written in the summer of

1998 for the journal *International Politics*. It remembers America's leadership after 1945 with, admittedly, some nostalgia—a postwar moment when America was in a "tell-me" mood: to lead was somewhat easier then than it is now, even if the evidence of vital U.S. interests could have been debated more seriously then than proved to be the case. After the Cold War, however, America now appears to be in a "show-me" mood. "Telling" the public what is to be done is no longer enough: explanations of the specific gains served by such action, whatever it may be, are also needed. This essay suggests that these explanations have been lacking during the past several years. In short, interests have been unveiled to justify the nation's commitments rather than the other way around—the unveiling of commitments justified by a specific set of interests. The essay, and the volume, therefore ends with hortatory tones: the case for internationalism need not be made timidly because the weight of the U.S. commitments it demands is reflective of the scope of the U.S. interests that these commitments are expected to protect and enhance.

One reason for presenting these essays in a single volume is that they form a whole that is less apparent if and when read separately, let alone selectively. Each essay paved the way for refining, stylistically and substantively, what had been written previously and what was to be written next. The compelling self-evident banality about Europe and its future is that there is more to Europe and its future than one issue only or one country only at a given time. Europe's single currency, admittedly the defining project of the coming years, is too important to be left to economists alone; elections in Germany, possibly the defining election of recent years, were too significant to be left exclusively to country watchers; and public anger at the erosion of national identity in many countries in Europe, arguably a defining issue for the next decade, is too important to be left to political sociologists. This is not a call for a superficiality that would justify a claim for instant expertise on all issues. Rather, this is one more warning against single-issue analysis. In short, the end of the Cold War has restored the primacy of the generalists over the specialists.

The passing of the Cold War has also meant the revenge of history over theory. Our fears of the future are shaped by our memories of the past and the meaning we give it. But aspirations for the future are also modified by such recollections and the significance we give them. On the eve of the twenty-first century, Europe's future is most reassuring if it is appraised retroactively: for what Europe ceased to be (or is still attempting to become in terms of completing its unity) and what it ceased to do (or resists adamantly with regard to the use of force) during the latter part of the twentieth century. Another reason for reproducing these essays is, therefore, a belief that the present is truly a defining moment for Europe—which means that Europe's future for much of the twenty-first century will be determined by the choices and the decisions made during this moment.

Because history likes to take its time, defining moments are usually few and lengthy. This defining moment, which is identifiable even as it unfolds, will not be long, however. The next few years may well suffice to decide whether the European Union has truly taken off, and whether this final phase in the construction of Europe can consecrate the final transformation of many separate nation-states into the member states of an ever more integrated European Union that takes over the sovereignty in the name of which so many wars were waged during the difficult history of the European continent.

As the states of Europe continue to wager that they have a future in the Union by giving the Union a future of its own, this is pay-off time for the EU: the planned emergence of the euro between 1999 and 2002 makes any pretense of coexistence between the two conditions of nation-state and member state especially adversarial and illusory. Thus, the like of French president Jacques Chirac's boast, in mid-1998, that he was committed to defending his country's national interest, during a dispute with German chancellor Helmut Kohl over the nomination of the first president of the European Central Bank, will not be repeated easily in coming years. If it is repeated, the new German chancellor, Gerhard Schroeder, may not hear it with the indulgence shown by his predecessor. If such indulgence persists, the new euro may not endure with the stability envisioned by the statesmen that gave it birth.

Now as before, it remains difficult to describe what might stand at the end of the process of European integration. What is known, however, is what stood at the beginning. Europe's past is the most effective reminder that during the Cold War the European states found, at last, the better way they needed for democratic stability, economic prosperity, and mutual security—better, that is, than any of the other ways they had followed during their long histories. Just imagine what would become of the European continent if the construction of Europe were to crash, amid the ruins of the euro, the failed attempts at institutional reform, or the frustrated hopes for a Common Foreign and Security Policy (CFSP) that begins with its long-promised enlargement to the east.

Underlining the case for the EU is also the fact that geography matters once again. After the Cold War, there is no longer room for small states whose urge for national grandeur would overcome their confining territorial space and shrinking populations. Abroad, there is no space left for these states to invade and conquer, as they once used to do—France moving south across the Mediterranean, Germany moving east into the Continent, and Britain moving in between and everywhere. Of this fact, at least, we can be sure. But at home, too, there is also not enough space available for the states of Europe to go it alone: the nation was their past, and Europe must now be their future.

This time, at last, most European countries west of Russia won this most recent (and also, hopefully, the last) global war waged in Europe: some countries, in the West, because of what they achieved during the time it took for them to win the Cold War, and others, in the East, because of the freedom they gained even while losing the Cold War. The new global war and the new local conflicts that loom ahead are being waged not between states and over boundaries, but within each state and over whatever remains of its territorial sovereignty. Leading these states to battle, political leaders are no longer what and who they used to be. Although the ghosts of past leaders may be sighted on the anniversary of the momentous events that they helped launch or whose triumph they helped ensure, these past leaders cannot be reborn in the guise of their successors. This, alas, is a farewell to the visions and leaders of yesteryear. Ambitions have taken precedence over convictions, and the will to succeed now, at this time, has replaced the urge to build over time.

Memories of past leadership feed our exasperation over tactical maneuvers that may compromise the future. Now, exit strategies, creative accounting, and imaginative spinning define one's ability to make decisions without having to make choices. Will the statesmen who brought the Cold War to closure remain the last statesmen whose vision of the present could still be conditioned by their apprehensions of the past and their aspirations for the future? To entertain memories of Europe's future is to state some relief that the past has been buried at last, but also to share a lingering concern over a future that refuses to be born.

PART ONE

Half Past NATO

1

Farewell to Yesteryear

TO BE BORN, AMERICA HAD TO LEAVE EUROPE; to grow in its new home, it had to live as an orphan; to mature as a great power, it had to visit its former relatives, although never for very long. Distance was a fact of geography but isolation was an act of national will, and neither distance nor isolation entailed indifference from one side of the Atlantic to the other. Europe was always the center of Americans' awareness of the world. Whether disdainful or apprehensive, they usually viewed the Continent through the prisms of temporary allies and enemies with and against which the United States won its wars, and with or in spite of which it attempted to win the peace.

In 1919, some historical virginity was cause for much misunderstanding. As America went home on the assumption that the job "over there" had been done, Europeans, too, returned to their old ways—or is it rather that as Europeans returned to their old ways, Americans went home? Whatever the explanation, the Old World was left with little protection from the prolonged wave of insanity that soon spread throughout and beyond the Continent. In 1945, the same mistake was not repeated. Americans had learned enough history to know that they could not leave, even if they did not understand fully what would become of them if they stayed as long as they ultimately did. Europe mattered enough, then, to avoid leaving it entirely to the Europeans—a conclusion also reached, although differently, by European colonial dependencies that were soon to rebel against a distant imperial rule, as America had 175 years earlier.

Now, there is little room for retrenchment. In their separate ways, Europeans and Americans are learning to bid farewell to their yesteryear. Two world wars prompted America to return to Europe, and one Cold War has made withdrawal impossible. For all the many differences that stand in the way of a true transatlantic community, Europe matters to Americans specifically because compatible ideals and converging self-interests are bridging the gap between the over there of the Old World and the over here of the New World. For all the bitterness of the past, Europe also matters to other regions of the world, old and new, because Europe's drive toward unity has taught these regions that they, too, can be relieved of the weight of their own history and the limits of their own geography.

Nothing lasts: the past is littered with countries, empires, and nations that came and went. Early in the twentieth century, the rise of American power came together with the collapse of Europe. More recently, exaggerated perceptions of declining American power, relative to that of friends and foes alike, conditioned the unveiling of rising powers in Asia and "new influentials" elsewhere. Power shifts are common in history. Late in the twentieth century, geography imposes its will over history, and economics takes precedence over politics. Too many wars waged by and between the countries of Europe have framed the collapse of societies whose most enduring memories are often bad and tragic. Cluttered with these mental cemeteries, the small pieces of real estate spread throughout the European continent are the stuff of the past. The nation-states of Europe are fading. Goodbye Europe? Bidding farewell to Europe is also tantamount to extending a belated welcome to "Europe" as an integrated union of states.

Still, Europe leaves little room for indifference because of both the good and the bad that Europeans have contributed and accomplished, over time as well as in the recent past. The cathedrals that are admired in awe rose as monuments to the sufferings of the multitudes that built them. Only when what stands before us can be admired all the more thoughtfully as the pain has died does the object of our admiration become visionary. So it is with Europe, a continent that might be worthy of our admiration because its past has finally died—along with a bellicose instinct that made its nations assume that whatever great things they could achieve would be even greater if they were achieved separately rather than in common.

As the century closes, its many ghosts are sighted, covered with the white sheets of a tragic history that refuses to end. No imagination is needed anymore: out of Bosnia and other places in and beyond Europe, television brings into the privacy of our homes the shocking pictures of death and starvation as we complete a plentiful dinner and prepare for a restful night. That, too, is part of Europe's legacy. The burden of empire remains heavy long after the empire is gone. Whether viewed as an imposition or as a mission, the civilization that the states of Europe used to export, across boundaries and across continents, was not always conducive to much civilized behavior.

But now that these empires have come home, they impose on the former mother countries a diversity that reflects their difficult and domineering history, including, alas, their unwillingness to accept the equality of all citizens irrespective of their origins. Because of their legacies, these empires also linger long after they ended, as debilitating memories of what "we" have ceased to be or as comforting expectations of who we no longer wish to become. The idea that "they" are and matter less, suggests that "we" matter more in the imagined communities with which we prefer to be identified.

Is there some lingering nostalgia for the past primacy of power over justice? Nationalist temptations remain, throughout the Continent and within many of its countries. Still, "that" Europe—arrogantly confident, brutally imperial, blindly self-destructive—is one that no longer matters and cannot be reborn. It died with an Austrian archduke in Sarajevo in 1914, when an entire generation was about to be denied the glorious gift of life for reasons, said to be of state, that every passing year has made look more unreasonable and, frankly, less human.

The killing goes on, to be sure, occasionally in the same places and even with the same primitive passions as in the past, but it is greeted elsewhere with exasperation and revulsion. Wherever they are, the great imperial powers of earlier ages have all bid farewell to their yesteryear: they no longer enter and wage war with the same spontaneity and exuberance as before. It is not civilization—what the French philosopher Henri Bergson used to call a "supplement of conscience"—that preempted such will to kill and willingness to be killed, but affluence. Ignore the facile analogies that warn against appeasement and the like, and forget the daunting memories that haunt our vision of the future: Europe's century of total wars has ended. Ironically, we must now acknowledge (although not always applaud) Europe's boredom with arms, and we can even accept (although not consequently rejoice) that a murderous conflict could erupt in one part of the European continent without causing an even more murderous conflict everywhere else.

From the Sarajevo that provided the catalyst for World War I to the Sarajevo that served as the symbol of a defeated new world order in Bosnia, Europe has come a long way. As we overcome our distaste for the daily horrors and repeated outrages that conditioned its journey through time and still occasionally intrude into our lives, we uncover the transformation of a large but fragmented space into an increasingly civil and integrated community whose people are learning how to live, reason, and act together. History has changed its ways, and geography has transformed its fragmented allure. As more and more European nation-states learn to abandon the prerogatives of their sovereignty to the benefit of the institutions to which many of them belong as member states, "Europe" becomes a unifying model that inspires other regions whose geography remains fragmented by a history whose tragedies must still be lived and endured.

In the end, the dismissal of Europe—does it matter!—is a measure of our ignorance of what has already been achieved, and of our impatience with what remains to be done. To appreciate Europe's current condition requires a retroactive logic that impels us to travel back in time and appraise it as what it has ceased to be, rather than as what it seems to be or what it might fail to become.

The Continent has awakened from its darkest hours to challenge the most enduring and least endearing concepts of politics. The urge for power and a natural instinct to seek dominance have given way to lasting democratic structures built by and for civil societies that are tired of war. Even history must have its statute of limitations, and Europe's ability to forget is a central feature of its capacity for renewal. The persistent calls for revenge and the lasting inclination to be blackmailed by national memories have been replaced by a collective amnesia that allows history to begin when postwar reconstruction ended and reconciliation began. The logic of cleavage and the sense of an exclusive identity asserted within the narrow boundaries of the nation-state have been overwhelmed by the logic of integration and the sense of unity that has transformed the nation-states of Europe into the member states of the European Union.

Admittedly, taking Europe and its ever closer Union seriously is not always easy. Divisions remain and fears linger. Yet, for the past five decades Europeans have taught the world that history can be made to change its course away from war, and that geography can be helped to change its ways without wars. Europe, in short, has become less than the many it used to be, although it remains more than the one it wishes to become. This is an example worth emulating for continents elsewhere, including Asia, where many of the great powers of the future are to be found, and in Africa, where there will remain many of the poorest states.

This century began, in Europe, many millions of lives ago, with much excitement and optimism. "A good time to be alive," said the poet Charles Péguy. We know about the collapse that followed, as well as the conditions of that collapse: Péguy died in war with the same passion he had brought into his poetry. That the century would be ending, again in Europe, with some gloom and pessimism need not be construed, therefore, as a final judgment about its irreversible demise. History has infinite imagination. The terms of the renewal that loom ahead for Europe, or the specific circumstances that will condition such renewal, may still be missing. Yet, we do know, already, that amid the ruins of many past decades of wars and civil conflicts stands a Europe that has never been as economically affluent, as politically stable, as widely united, and as deeply peaceful as it is today.

That such would be the case is a tribute to the policies the United States launched, or helped launch, in and for Europe. They represent the most enduring memories of leadership that the new generations of Americans should and will inherit for the next century. For those whose impatience with the pace of change in Europe is cause for exasperation and despair, and for those whose intolerance of the lingering burdens of power and leadership makes them question whether Europe still matters, the capacity for unity and self-renewal demonstrated over the past 50 years is evidence of relevance and reason for hope.

2

Years of Europe

M UCH THAT HAPPENED IN EUROPE since the Cold War ended serves as a reminder that every postwar configuration is by definition fraught with uncertainties and beset with instabilities. However dramatic the recovery of Europe's nation-states has been since 1945, the European Union (EU) is still unfinished and the European continent is still divided; and however weary America may be of the role it assumed after World War II, its leadership and power remain indispensable. These "lessons" were all known but conveniently ignored in the euphoria that followed the momentous events of the early 1990s. In the United States at least, they must be addressed in the context of three questions: Why care, what next, and who leads?

Why Care?

Should Americans care about the fate of a continent they abandoned more than 200 years ago? Does Europe matter? That these questions would need to be asked is puzzling. That there would be some resistance to responding unequivocally is troubling. The case for U.S. involvement in Europe is based on American interests. Failure to make that case suggests a willingness to make the case for isolation because no other part of the world except, arguably, the Western Hemisphere can claim the same complete relationship that prevails across the Atlantic. This relationship involves

- regional security interests shaped in Europe by two dominant nation-states, Russia and Germany, each unsure of the other and both feared by their neighbors;

- the geopolitical interest of adding Europe's power to that of the United States to address new global issues and face rising great powers in other parts of the world, including but not limited to Asia;

- a full range of economic transactions that extend beyond commercial transactions, and that face less discord and more regulated rivalry with each passing year;

- societal interests and values that are not always common but that the U.S. and European democracies share more and more visibly with each other than with any other region.

In short, the Cold War has done what neither world war could: U.S. interests in Europe have become so significant as to make disengagement neither possible nor meaningful. Differences remain, to be sure, some old and others yet to come. Yet, however dramatic they may look at any time, these differences are now small compared to the commonality of interests that bridge the two sides of an increasingly common Euro-American space.

Within that space, national sovereignty has been losing much of its past relevance. As nation-states learn to live, however reluctantly, with their new constraints, the North Atlantic Treaty Organization (NATO) and the European Union are the two main institutions that define that space (with others, like the World Trade Organization, helping place that space within a more global environment). Both institutions were born out of commitments made by the United States and the states of Europe to save them from the recurrence of past European excesses. Although these commitments were different, they were both compatible and complementary. The end of the Cold War may have weakened the case for either or both of these institutions, and the commitments that underlie them, but it did not end the case for either. To argue otherwise is to forget the reasons that gave them birth after two world wars (and before the Cold War). Now and for the years to come, the instabilities that characterize the post–Cold War conditions in Europe are not the consequences of the Cold War. Rather, they are the deferred consequences of pre- and post-World War II conditions that were poorly addressed in 1919 and forced into the cage of ideological confrontation after 1945.

The EU remains a very important U.S. interest, if for no other reason than it is a vital interest for the states of Europe. Moreover, it is also a direct U.S. interest because it has served, and continues to serve, U.S. interests exceptionally well:

- the prosperity of a united Europe helps keep America affluent;

- the stability of a democratic Europe helps strengthen American values; and

- the security of war-weary European states helps protect America from the risks of another major war in Europe that it would deplore but from which it could not escape.

Because U.S. policies still influence the construction of Europe—directly or indirectly—decisions that reinforce the fact or even the perception of U.S. commitment to a strong and united Europe are desirable. Conversely, demonstrations of hostility or even ambivalence about a process to which U.S. contributions were decisive in the past must be carefully avoided. When dealing with Europe, U.S. officials face an especially difficult intellectual challenge: to end a tendency to fragment space and isolate time—a tendency, that is, to address countries and issues one at a time and from time to time. This tendency has become much worse since the end of the Cold War unleashed old historical forces and threatened new geographic pressures.

The completion of an integrated Europe as a genuine political union extended to the totality of the European continent is in the interest of the United States, but it is not a U.S. responsibility. It is the responsibility of the EU's members. Clearly, EU membership is a status which the United States neither holds nor expects. More effective means of consultation between the United States and the EU should prevail, so that the special status of the United States as a major power in Europe (but not as a European power) can be acknowledged. Admittedly, however, not any sort of Europe will do, and U.S. support applies, therefore, to a European Union that is specifically

- open, flexible, and competitive in economic structure and practice;

- democratic and compatible with social values and policies that prevail in the United States;

- resistant to protectionist pressures exerted by EU institutions or advocated by some of its members for selected industrial and growth sectors;

- open to economic and political ties with the East, starting with Central Europe; and

- able to assume a larger share of the defense burden, with a Western European Union (WEU) responsive to the need for a special relationship with the United States within NATO.

This latter requirement holds an imperative of its own. NATO is the most visible and easily recognizable institutional tie between America and Europe. In the absence of a suitable alternative, NATO remains, therefore, the primary tool available to the United States to

- maintain a military presence in Europe that can help deter an outburst of Russian geopolitical revisionism, which is not likely but remains possible;

- guarantee the security of the former Warsaw Pact countries—not because of any explicit threat but because there are risks of instabilities exported or manipulated by their neighbors;

- consolidate Germany's confidence, as well as that of other states throughout Europe, in a Western security structure that is more reliable and certainly less controversial than any alternative;

- deter, settle, and possibly defend against small conflicts in and even out of Europe, where Western interests can and do converge; and

- prepare for, and respond to, common global issues that concern societies on both sides of the Atlantic, including terrorism, environmental degradation, and the proliferation of weapons of mass destruction.

Public confusion in the United States over NATO enlargement from 16 to 19 members (and more) results, at best, from the fact that the case made on its behalf has been too narrow. Such a case, it should be clear, is

- not about NATO enlargement but about NATO itself because a failure by the United States to seek enlargement, and by the U.S. Senate to ratify that decision, would probably have undermined NATO to the point of irrelevance;

- not about NATO but about the U.S. role in Europe, because lacking NATO, the United States would have no readily available conduit for exerting its leadership and sustaining its power in Europe;

- not about Europe but about U.S. interests in Europe, because these interests are too significant to be left to Europeans whose projects of unity are too ambitious to be completed any time soon; and

- not just about the U.S. role and interests in Europe but also about the U.S. role and interests in the world, because much that involves Europe and U.S.-European relations spills over on the rest of the world.

What Next?

Taking the idea of Europe seriously can be demanding. The seriousness of European integration has to do with the tangible reality acquired by the institutions built since the end of World War II. For their members, there is no turning back; for the many countries that are now applying for membership, there is no alternative. Nevertheless, the truth of claims that "Europe" has come too far to change course and reopen the door to past conflicts is not self-evident. Risks of violent conflict abound, and bad habits linger—more now than at any time since the Rome Treaties were signed in 1957.

After World War II, the integration of Europe was conditioned originally by a will to accept some restraints on national sovereignty in return for tangible gains that would help the states of Europe to overcome their national limitations. After the Cold War, further integration appears hampered by a blend of failed expectations and growing public skepticism. To many in the United States, but also in Europe, the state of the EU is all the more fragile as the governments of its members object to the loss of their sovereignty and their respective constituencies rebel against the erosion of their identity. The political volatility in Europe since the Cold War has to do, among other reasons, with the economic rigor and political discipline imposed on each state in the name of the EU, and with a more fundamental resistance to an ideological and social convergence achieved at the expense of some heroic myths about who and what a given group used to be. In any case, under prevailing conditions, no nation-state in Europe can lead alone (not even, and perhaps least of all, Germany), and EU members are too divided for any one of them to pretend to lead in their name (not even, and perhaps least of all, France).

That Americans would be exasperated with such conditions in Europe reflects an especially poor understanding of the immense scope and complexity of the EU agenda. Now as before, parts of this agenda seem to lie beyond the reach of the EU. Yet, every EU claim that is not met on time need not be viewed as evidence that it will not be met later. Thus, between 1999 and 2005 the EU states must

- agree on the institutional reforms that 18 months of intergovernmental negotiations failed to resolve prior to the summit of the European Council held in Amsterdam in June 1997;

- make and enforce painful decisions about the euro, between 1999 and 2002, decisions that might prove to be so painful as to precipitate serious political debates about the EU in each member state (as well as between them);

- welcome several new members from the east, but also at the periphery of the Continent (like Malta and Cyprus) and develop association agreements with countries farther east (including Ukraine) and with regions farther south (including North Africa).

These issues are not new. In the past, each stood in the way of European unity until it was settled with last-minute compromises or, when disagreement could not be overcome, with a *relance* (relaunching) of the institutions over some other issue. What is new, however, is that all items on the agenda must be addressed simultaneously: widen in order to deepen, deepen in order to widen, and reform in order to do both.

Adding to the complexity of the EU agenda are questions of intra-European leadership. Over the past four decades, the leadership of Europe may have been voiced by one single European state but it never was, or could be, enforced by one state alone. Bilateral relations, therefore, have been especially significant as the engine that made Europe move—with or without the United States, with more or less unity. Since the end of the Cold War, however, these bilateral relations have become unusually fluid, especially between the three European states (France, Germany, and Great Britain) that have been most directly responsible for the evolution of Western Europe since 1945.

Thus, the Franco-German relationship that has helped "define" Europe since 1945 is more tenuous than at any time since Charles de Gaulle and Konrad Adenauer first met in Rambouillet, near Paris, in September 1958. From one German chancellor to the next, and while awaiting the next French president, bilateral differences between these two countries can be all the more significant as Bonn becomes less willing to make the concessions that Paris has become used to as a matter of tradition. In 1999 and beyond, German emphasis on budgetary discipline and a strong president for the European Central Bank, and the French insistence that these objectives and their commitments be balanced by the need to promote growth and protect jobs, will test the language of the "stability pact" Bonn and Paris painfully negotiated and signed in December 1996. Such a test might then go beyond what a new German chancellor would be willing to agree, but below what a new French president would be able to accept.

Other Franco-German bilateral strains abound: an agonizing reappraisal of majority voting in the European Council and the reallocation of seats (no more than one) in the European Commission, new trade negotiations (dubbed the Millennium Round) and new reforms of the Common Agricultural Policy (CAP), privileged ties with former dependencies in the south to parallel closer ties with former adversaries in the east, the pace of reform for achieving a Common Foreign and Security Policy (CFSP), and the formula that may be adopted for the integration of the Western European Union in the EU. These are all issues, among many others, about which French differences with a minimalist Great Britain become smaller while differences with a maximalist Germany seem to grow larger.

The change of government in Great Britain in May 1997 opened the door wider to the first lasting Anglo-French rapprochement in the history of the Fifth Republic. Such a rapprochement, should it continue, would parallel France's increasing ambivalence about its role in an ever-more-united Europe (an ambivalence that could worsen as political posturing begins to shape the next French presidential election, in the year 2002 or before) and Britain's more constructive European policy with a "new" Labour Party that has been learning to like the EU ever since its humiliating electoral defeat of 1983. Closer relations between London and Paris, combined with improved relations of London (let alone Paris) with Washington, would provide the intercontinental link, across the Atlantic and across the Channel, that has been missing since the United States denied France and Britain during the 1956 Suez crisis, since Britain refused to sign the 1957 Rome Treaties, and since the 1958 Gaullist call for a NATO directoire with London and Washington (but without Germany).

Postwar restraints accepted by the states of Europe during much of the Cold War, vis-à-vis each other within the EU (when agreeing to the inclusion of Germany in the postwar plans for reconstruction, for example) and vis-à-vis the United States within NATO (when agreeing to an often assertive and demanding leadership), originally resulted from three factors. First, there was the evidence of failure: namely, that the European wars of the twentieth century had amounted to a suicidal pact that had to be ended. Such evidence had been viewed as insufficient after 1919, when some states in Europe could claim they had "won" the war; it was deemed compelling in 1945, when no such claim could be made by any West European state (with the possible exception of Britain). Then, there was the Soviet factor as the originator of a new European balance that had not existed since Germany's unification in 1871 and had not been feared since Napoleon's defeat in 1815. That factor, too, was not central to post–World War I conditions only two years after the newly established and weak revolutionary government in Moscow had signed a painful separate peace with Germany in Brest-Litovsk. Finally, there was the factor of American power, benign enough to be trusted and assertive enough to be respected.

Acceptance of these restraints caused expectations of two types of gains. First, there were expectations of growth and affluence, which did reward the ever larger number of European states that lent their sovereignty to NATO and the EU. Second, expectations of collective security and individual safety were combined with the assumption that Europeans would still preserve a credible sense of their own identity and values relative to each other as well as to the United States.

Today, however, these restraints and expectations have been replaced with two recriminations. First, the countries of Europe are unhappy with their limits—what they can do alone or as a union, with the help of the state or against it. This condition is especially deplored as crises over which they have no control (like an economic meltdown in Asia) threaten to affect decisions they do control (like the decision to launch the euro). Second, there are mounting objections to the loss of national identities within the European community, and of a European identity within the Atlantic community. Although both sides of the Atlantic and all sides in the EU show compelling evidence of converging views in national and international affairs, their people often seem to speak of different things while using the same words in the second language (English) that has become common to all of them.

Whatever the conditions of the public debate, it aims mainly at the all-absorbing issue of Economic and Monetary Union (EMU). Forget the aspirations of the single market, the costs of enlargement, the tragedies of Bosnia, the delusions of a common security identity, and the frustrations over America's power and leadership. Forget all that and more: as EMU goes during the little time left before the end of the twentieth century, so will the EU during the years that will open the twenty-first century. Yet, even as 11 EU members launch the euro as a substitute for their national currencies, with most other members prepared to join later, the nation-states of Europe and their constituencies are growing more rebellious. As was the case with the European Monetary System (EMS) after 1979, the EMU debate will continue in the streets and the marketplace between 1999 and 2002, when European currencies are scheduled to lose whatever might remain of their status as legal tenders. How well the resulting monetary and political turbulence is faced, and how effectively the euro helps relaunch job creation in Europe, will affect public attitudes toward the EU and, therefore, public approval of the EU's relentless drive to an ever deeper union, including political union, and a wider union, including the admission of new members.

That the "perceived distance between the Union and its citizens" that was "stressed" by the European Commission in its *Agenda 2000* would have become wider than the distance among EU governments suggests that there might come a time when pressures from the citizens could force some of these governments to change course. A "Europe" that is increasingly viewed as a consumer of affluence (whether earned by the citizen or granted by the *état providence*) and as a producer of painful austerity can be politically costly for those who associate their fate with the promises of more, not less, union. In early 1997, Helmut Kohl's tears at François Mitterrand's funeral were shed for a dying generation of European statesmen, including Kohl himself, no less than for the late French president. Throughout continental Europe, many of the emerging national leaders poised to compete for the highest office in their respective countries now show an ambivalence about

Europe that would have disqualified them in the past from such lofty ambitions. As dissent from Europe emerges as an effective path to power, the temptation to move in that direction may become irresistible even if it is widely understood that there can be no alternative to staying with and in Europe once in power.

In the past, disaffection from the European Community reflected the ideological cleavage within the Left (between Communists and Socialists) and the Right (between moderates and extreme nationalists)—as was the case most vividly in France and Italy. Where there was little or no Communist Party, as was the case in Germany and Britain, the cleavage was more directly between a conservative Right and a Socialist Left that complained of Europe's predilection for the marketplace at the expense of labor. Now, however, such a generalization can no longer suffice in any one of the EU countries because there is no Cold War to justify it, no Left-Right cleavage to guide it, and no *projet de société* to motivate it. Paradoxically, since the collapse of communism and the disintegration of the Soviet Union, the political mood in Europe has moved back to the Left: now, the first Labour government in Britain since 1979 and the first Social-Democrat chancellor in Germany since 1983 merely await the next French presidential election to form the first troika of leftist governments in these three countries since World War II.

If nothing else, this trend confirms how difficult it was for leftist political parties to live in the shadow of an inept and brutal regime in Moscow. Liberated at last from the ugly face of Soviet communism, the European Left is effective because it no longer has to be revolutionary: no need for a "new society" because there is no other society and there can be, therefore, no other "program" than avoiding the pain that goes with "Europe." So, the electoral promises of the Left echo the political regrets of the Right. Ask not what Tony Blair or Lionel Jospin, and Gerhard Schroeder or Massimo d'Alema, will be able to do for their country; ask rather what John Major and Jacques Chirac, and Helmut Kohl or Romano Prodi, will have failed to do—like protecting and creating jobs, or providing for and protecting the nation's identity.

Who Leads?

Questions in the United States about Europe's followership are not new. Yet, for Europeans to ask for more time to act in completing their union and attending to their responsibilities in and beyond Europe sounds too much like an excuse for another free ride through the vicissitudes of postwar instabilities. This may not be Europe's time yet, but these are the years during which Europe's decisions will be down payments on what else may be coming in later years. Three examples will suffice:

- The two processes of EU and NATO enlargement are separate, but the logic of doing the latter while awaiting the former is neither convincing nor reassuring;

- U.S. forces will remain in Bosnia indefinitely, announced President William Clinton in late 1997, but a European identity that echoes U.S. decisions ("You stay, therefore we choose not to leave") is neither credible nor sufficient;

- The United States should pay a fair share of NATO enlargement, but Europe's logic of refusing to pay for a so-called American idea is not acceptable either, coming from countries whose security could not be sustained, or at least not as cheaply, without NATO.

As Americans raise questions about Europe's followership, Europeans are not averse to raising questions about U.S. leadership. These questions, too, are hardly new. The states of Europe have always feared hegemonic power—except their own; and they have always feared a U.S. penchant for unilateral action—except when they thought they had cause for bemoaning America's instinct for disengagement. Now as before, the U.S. leadership is said to be "arrogant"—meaning, reflexive, hazardous, futile, and deceptive: reflexive because it is explicitly sensitive to domestic political pressures; hazardous because the cost of U.S. failures must often be borne by Europe because of its dissymmetrical security relationship with America; futile because it is not sensitive to the long-term trends history teaches; and deceptive because it all too often speaks with the language of principles that clash with the self-interests that motivate many of its actions.

Nonetheless, the end of the Cold War has left the United States with an unprecedented blend of military dominance (the power to compel), economic self-sufficiency (the power to ignore), political influence (soft power), and global reach (structural power). The absence of a challenger to the post–Cold War power of the United States is unlikely to endure indefinitely, but in the absence of a clear challenger, the most compelling limitation on U.S. power is based on factors of self-denial: a lack of will—the will to use military force, the tolerance for pain and the will to inflict it.

To return to the uniqueness of American history as an explanation of such self-denial is banal but true. America's relations with the world have been distant, and its relationship with Europe is still viewed by many as unnatural—a blind date with a distant relative that has turned into a lasting arrangement. Yet, on the whole, America's forays into Europe have turned out quite well—usually better than anywhere else—and what is remembered from them is cause for public satisfaction and even celebration.

Now, too, there should be much cause for celebration. But too little of that celebration is heard on either side of the Atlantic. What is heard instead, especially in the United States, involves mainly single-issue polemics that have hijacked policy debates: over the unpredictability of Russia's future, for example, first after Mikhail Gorbachev and then after Boris Yeltsin; over the joys of a postwar peace dividend but, later, the imperative of renewed defense spending; over staying out of Bosnia when the war raged and staying in Bosnia after the war ended; over NATO dissolution and, next, NATO enlargement to 19 and more members.

The pattern that is therefore established is self-deceptive and destructive: self-deceptive because it pretends an ability to address one issue at a time, and destructive because it leaves no time for any one issue. The post–World War II history of transatlantic relations, and of European integration as well, has been a history of discord and cooperation, with the latter easily gaining and holding the advantage over the former. More specifically, the most consistent, most successful, and most rewarding U.S. foreign policy launched since the end of World War II was in Europe. What has been achieved during this relatively short period of time (by historical standards) is extraordinary. In a civil space that now covers half of the Continent, nations that used to wage war on each other have changed their ways. The rewards of unity—affluence, stability, and security—have been shared by all partners on both sides of the Atlantic, including the United States.

To abandon Europe to itself would be to ignore these achievements at a huge cost to U.S. interests. As a new century begins, the availability of U.S. power and leadership to manage the current transition and help begin a new millennium with an enthusiasm justified further by the obvious rarity of such occurrences is not tied to any certainty over what such power and leadership will in fact achieve during the coming years, but, rather, to the certainty of what has been achieved to date. After the Cold War, America has too many interests in Europe not to care and not to lead as Europe moves forward toward becoming whole and free.

3

Steadfast and Changing

T HE POST–COLD WAR YEARS ARE OVER. The years since the reintegration of the two Germanys into one, and the disintegration of the Soviet Union into many, have been less demanding than the years after 1919, when the flawed postwar system emerged only in the aftermath of the ill-fated French occupation of the Ruhr, or than after 1945, when the postwar structure began to take form with the signing of the Washington Treaty and the subsequent establishment of the North Atlantic Treaty Organization (NATO). As NATO's fiftieth anniversary is celebrated with the enlargement of the North Atlantic security area to three new members from Central Europe, the future is about to begin.

But what future—a resurrection of the worst and most tragic features of the distant past or a celebration of the best legacies of a more recent past? The evidence gathered to date is not conclusive. As should have been expected from a moment of geopolitical transition, the post–Cold War years in Europe were fraught with instabilities and uncertainty. These were seen most visibly and most painfully in the Balkans, including but not limited to Bosnia and the rest of what used to be known as Yugoslavia. Instabilities and uncertainties in Europe have to do, too, with future conditions in what used to be known as the Soviet Union, including Russia, the defeated state, but also many of the countries that fell under its domination before and after the 1917 revolution. On the whole, however, the main features of post–Cold War Europe are not the exclusive consequences of the Cold War. Instead, the unity achieved in the West and the degradation uncovered in the East can be related more directly to the legacies of earlier wars, including the two world wars that conditioned the distribution of power in and beyond Europe during much of the twentieth century.

As a result of these instabilities, the debate over the post–Cold War future of NATO has proven to be stillborn. With the postwar expectations of stability quickly exhausted, calls for new structures that would substitute for wartime alliances quickly stopped. The Organization for Cooperation and Security in Europe (OCSE), whose wide membership, including both the United States and Russia, made it look like the most promising alternative to NATO, gained a new name and then disappeared as the earlier need for a constructive role of Russia in Europe began to fade. For a short while after 1989, calls for a dissolution of NATO were heard too, mainly from those who had been making the same calls during the Cold War. Since 1993, however, these calls have become less frequent, and the centrality of the alliance has ceased to be challenged at a time that is, at most, half-past-NATO. Concomitantly, expectations of a quick and full completion of the European construction have lost the intensity they had after the Maastricht Treaty was signed in December 1991. Instead, the war in Bosnia has confirmed that this is not Europe's time after all, whether for its individual nation-states or for the European Union (EU) to which 15 of them already belong, with several more to come. At best, the time is half-before-Europe, pending Europe's ability to take further and better care of its security needs.

Nor are serious questions raised any longer over the centrality of the U.S. role and power within NATO, and hence in post–Cold War Europe. If anything, compared to the aftermath of either one or both of the previous two world wars, there have been fewer calls for a return home, fewer indications of a collapse or a fragmentation of the victorious wartime alliance, and fewer indications of new bids from either the defeated states or new contenders for regional or global hegemony. In 1998, the debate in the U.S. Senate over the ratification of NATO enlargement could have raised some echoes of the Senate debate over U.S. membership in the League of Nations nearly 80 years earlier. Yet, memories of that debate and its outcome helped avoid whatever potential there was for a replay of the past.

The legacy left from the long reprieve from history imposed by the Cold War is especially sound in the western half of the Continent. The legacy, there, is that of a new European space that has been modified by the five major events that have changed the established course of Europe's history: the collapse of colonial empires; the erosion of the nation-state; the end of the Left-Right cleavage; the de-legitimation of war; and the return of the New World into the Old.

Considered separately, these changes are well known. The colonial wars that erupted after the two world wars consecrated the collapse of Europe. More pointedly, they provided a global setting in which East-West conflicts could be staged at the least cost for its two main protagonists, and also served frequently as a catalyst for discord in transatlantic and intra-European relations. The Left-Right cleavages had been a recurring source of serious domestic instabilities for each European state since the turn of the century. They also became an invitation for destabilizing political intrusions from without after 1945—from the Soviet Union, to be sure, but also from the United States, whose involvement in the internal politics of European states was especially significant during the formative years of the Cold War. After enlightened European political leaders understood the need to force Europe's nationalisms into a cage loosely called "Europe," a growing number of countries came to accept a collective discipline that challenged their national sovereignty.

Throughout much of the Continent, Europe's taste for armed conflicts, too, soured after the orgy of violence endured during both world wars, but also because of the impotence shown during the subsequent years of the Cold War when the states of Europe could neither gain their autonomy nor regain their independence, let alone whatever control they used to hold over distant lands. Finally, the postwar U.S. decision to stay in Europe, which defined Europe after 1945, proved to be far more entangling than the Truman administration had envisioned, both during the Cold War when U.S. commitments grew steadily and since the Cold War when these commitments could no longer be reversed.

These developments were all linked, but how these linkages worked has not been discussed as fully as the ways in which each emerged and unfolded separately. For example, after the small states of Europe had lost their empires abroad, their quest for additional space took the more civil form of European integration.

Thus, the colonial wars ended about when a small European Community was launched and the political wars within each of its six initial members began to recede. Between 1958 and 1963 came years of significant domestic political changes in France (emergence of the Fifth Republic), Germany (transition after Chancellor Konrad Adenauer), and Italy (opening of the Christian Democratic majority to the non-Communist Left). Next, the sense of an ever larger European "community" of states, coupled with the rise of affluence and the end of debilitating colonial conflicts, helped delegitimize the use of force both from within and from without Europe. Such new prosperity and stability among the allies in turn emerged as an open invitation for the United States to reduce its postwar obligations and achieve a more equitable sharing of the many burdens of the West, whether in defending its security and values against Soviet power and ideology in the East or in extending its interests and influence in the newly independent South.

The Empires Come Home

As the century ends, sustaining the changes that have conditioned the transformation of Europe since the century began will present a defining challenge for the years to come. A reversal of the conditions found especially in Western Europe after 50 years of cold war could take different forms. For the countries at the periphery of the Continent, there is little danger, of course, of the European states attempting to rebuild their empires in Africa or in Asia—at least not by force. Those days are over. Still, whether as providers of attractive economic opportunities or as sources of serious security risks, countries in the South will continue to play a central role in the life of much of Europe, as well as in Europe's relations with the United States and even Russia. This role could be especially important on the southern shores of the Mediterranean, where an arc of Islamic crises extends from Algeria and the balance of North Africa and farther south into Nigeria, through the Middle East and the Persian Gulf, to Turkey and the Muslim republics of the defunct Soviet Union.

The return home of Europe's old empires can follow many paths. Most evident is the path drawn by groups of immigrants intent on leaving the harsh economic and political conditions that prevail in their respective countries to settle in the former mother country or some of its neighbors in a broad and affluent Europe opened by agreements that were designed to abolish frontiers. Alternatively, former imperial dependencies can export to the former mother countries either economic scarcities with a manipulation of the price and supply of vital commodities (such as oil), or sheer violence with terrorism and the like—with either export being the source of dangerous political instabilities.

In either of these conditions, the question of Islam in Europe—a question distinct from, but admittedly related to, the broader question of Europe and Islam—raises a significant, possibly decisive, challenge to European security. Relations with Islam have been experienced in Europe differently than in the United States, and they are still lived differently not only from one side of the Atlantic to the other, but also from one European state to another. After 1999, this challenge could quickly become internal even more than external, as the threats raised by the radicalization of an Islamic diaspora within many European states (whether secular, like France, or not, like Great Britain) could rely on potential ties with the radical Islamic states abroad.

More broadly, Europe's relations with Islam, and Islam's relations with Europe, affect political trade-offs and bargains within the EU: important issues like the allocation of structural subsidies to EU regions that remain underdeveloped, but also the whole question of EU enlargement to Eastern Europe (relative to an alleged neglect of other regions outside Europe), fall into the new North-South tension that divides the EU at 15. Finally, in a growing number of cases, how to deal with Islamic revolutionary states is a question that significantly affects Europe's relations with the United States, and even Russia. Examples include the Persian Gulf (over the U.S. strategy of "dual containment" relative to Europe's preference for "constructive dialogue") and the Middle East (over the U.S. approach to the Arab-Israeli peace process or even state-sponsored terrorism).

Already during the Cold War, issues of empire often widened the Left-Right cleavage in each of the European countries that endured the agony of decolonization and withdrawal. Predictably, internal differences between political parties were also exacerbated in periods of East-West tensions, relative to occasional bursts of détente between the United States and the Soviet Union. Yet, the end of empires and the end of the Cold War do not mean the end of political divisions and hence, the end of political and even regime instabilities. Historically, cleavages within the Left and within the Right have often been as significant as the Left-Right cleavage. Now, however, the collapse of communism has given the Socialist Left a new lease on life in the largest European states: in Britain and Italy first (with Tony Blair's "New Labour" and Romano Prodi's "Olive Tree" coalition with the former Communist Party) and in France and Germany next (with Lionel Jospin's revived Socialists and Gerhard Schroeder's renewed Social Democrats). Europe's non-Communist Left is all the more at ease in this new political environment because it no longer needs to be revolutionary. Compassion for the unemployed sells well, and claims of competence are especially convincing if and when these claims are made relative and in opposition to the insufficiencies of those in power.

For the extreme Right, the collapse of the Soviet Union restores prospects for a political legitimacy denied by its conservative competitors because of the Cold War against totalitarianism. Boasting of an assertive nationalism may no longer be as "bad" as might have been the case earlier. In countries like Austria and France, the extreme Right commands between one-sixth and one-fourth of the electorate. In Italy, a reborn neo-Fascist party has regained legitimacy with a dynamic new leader, Gianfranco Fini, who contends for national leadership. In this case, too, Germany might be next as it unloads the debilitating burdens of uniqueness and rediscovers a past that a postwar generation of Germans had previously learned to master by pretending that Germany had no past. This temptation is especially strong in the eastern part of the country, where the collapse of communism has not been conducive to the prosperity that had been initially anticipated. In short, it is not only the Cold War that ended in the 1990s: so did World War II. "Helmut Kohl's generation," pointedly noted Gerhard Schroeder in a BBC interview in late March 1998, "thinks Germans must be part of Europe to prevent Europe from being frightened by Germany in the future. . . . My generation believes that Germans don't have to be part of Europe, but we want to be." Whether this might be construed as a promise reflective of what has changed in Europe, or as a warning reminiscent of what has remained steadfast, is yet to be seen.

As Europe moves into a new century, such political volatility could take a heavy toll. The 1997 legislative elections in France, which were held in part because of the EU calendar for monetary union, confirmed that challenges to the discipline of Europe work at the expense of political leaders who associate their political fate with the promises of more, not less, Europe. Yet, after a new majority had been elected, Jospin could find no alternative to going along with the policies to which he had objected: dissenting from Europe can show the way to power even if no alternative to Europe can be found once in power. In France as in the other core countries that signed the Rome Treaties in 1957, including Germany, the conditions of a future populist challenge to the idea of Europe may be emerging.

Clashes within the two sides of the political spectrum and between them risk fragmenting the current consensus and provoking public outbursts of anger aimed not only at the EU (and NATO too) but also at the constitutional frameworks that helped achieve political stability during the Cold War. In some cases, the constitutional risk is to do nothing. This is the case in France, where political cohabitation between President Jacques Chirac and Prime Minister Lionel Jospin until the end of Chirac's seven-year term in 2002 would erode the presidential identity of the regime defined by the 1962 constitution, and thus end the Fifth Republic as it has been known since de Gaulle. In other cases, as in Italy, the risk is over doing something, like a constitutional reform that would launch a presidential regime that gives precedence to charisma *à l'italienne* (i.e., that of the neo-Fascist Fini) over competence *à l'américaine* (i.e., that of the neo-centrist Prodi).

Whatever the changes, they will happen around "Europe" as the defining political issue. For now the intrusion of the European

Union into the day-to-day lives of each nation-state can best motivate the new ideologues who complain of the state's inability to
protect the citizens from the market, and the nation's identity from
the Union.

In a narrow sense, the EU is the victim of its agenda: too much
Europe has been hurting it. The EU suffers from an agenda over-
load whose rigid timetable carries dangers of derailment with every
delay or setback: the euro in January 1999, when the EU states will
begin a three-year farewell to their national currencies; another
InterGovernmental Conference (IGC) in or around the year 2001,
when the 15 EU members will address issues of institutional governance that they failed to settle when IGC-96 was concluded in
June 1997; and enlargement by 2003, when the EU should be
ready to begin its expansion to the East. The scope, complexity,
and significance of this agenda are unprecedented. In every
instance and for all 15 members, the EU will cost a lot of money,
will take away a lot of sovereignty, and will impose a lot of austerity. In short, the EU now promises to create a lot of pain that will
cause a lot of public resentment.

In a broader sense, the EU is also victimized by its own successes. Nonmembers view it as a shortcut to economic prosperity and
democratic stability. Members continue to view it as a recipe for
affluence at home and influence abroad. The latter's growing resistance to the financial and political costs of integration, combined
with the former's growing awareness of the parallel costs of membership, give the process unprecedented fragility because of what
current members are willing to concede relative to what applicants
are forced to demand.

The erosion of Europe's permissive consensus about its Union
is all the more significant as there seem to be no political leaders
capable of either protecting the EU against its members or defending the nation-state against the Union. For the past 40 years, whenever community building in Europe carried a cost (meaning,
economic dislocations or erosion of sovereignty), that cost could be
contained with vocal national leaders (whether General de Gaulle
in the 1960s or Margaret Thatcher in the 1980s) who spoke on
behalf of the skeptics, or with new institutions (like the European

Council and even the European Parliament in the late 1970s) that restored the primacy of the national governments and their respective publics.

Now, in the 1990s, the reassuring voices of dissent cannot be found as readily, and the new institutional arrangements are more difficult to launch too. When it comes to Europe, the political leaders of all three leading EU countries have a checkered past—be it Blair, whose "discovery" of the EU is relatively new, or Jospin and Schroeder, who can hardly boast of the same European convictions as their predecessors within their political family (Mitterrand and Helmut Schmidt) or in the country (Chirac and Kohl). Worse yet, as the euro takes hold, no institutional gimmick is going to hide the further erosion of a national sovereignty left at the mercy of a European Central Bank that will give the Europeans a single voice without which economic and monetary union can be launched but cannot succeed.

A mixture of economic and cultural crisis—meaning, uncertainties over affluence and identity—has never been healthy for Europe. Now, however, the countries of Europe lack the means and the will to fight together as a union of states, or to fight alone or, mercifully, with each other. Plans for a more cohesive and stronger Western European Union (WEU) should be encouraged by the United States, but for many years to come these plans will remain an aspiration more than a reality. The war in Bosnia could have been the catalyst for the development of WEU, but the war proved to be too demanding militarily under conditions that were too distracting politically.

As in the United States, the mood in Europe is inward and the interests are self-centered. In 1998 and for a few years before, the focus of EU attention was on EMU. In 1999 and for several years after, EMU will remain the center of EU attention. Paradoxically, however, a derailment of monetary union could create such institutional urgency for a quick relaunch of Europe as to benefit a Common Foreign and Security Policy (CFSP)—as was the case when collapse of the European Defense Community in late 1954 was the catalyst for the decision to relaunch Europe with an economic community that was to be based on the more modest idea of a Common Market.

To be sure, even a CFSP launch after 1999, whatever form that decision might take, would still leave any credible common *security* policy postponed for many more years, pending the resolution of numerous and complex institutional issues. Yet, in the intervening years, there can be a common *foreign* policy, which is the policy adopted and enforced in common by the 15 EU countries and designed to achieve enlargement to the East at the earliest possible time.

America Comes Home

Finally, the future of the Cold War legacies in Western Europe is related to the future of U.S. involvement in Europe, and its will to stay on the Continent that a fading majority of Americans used to call home. Some still view the fact or even the mere perception of an American withdrawal, whatever form it might take, as a catalyst for action. The argument is not new. In the 1960s, too, calls for a withdrawal of U.S. forces were made to force the Europeans to assume a larger share of their own defense. Yet, now as before, a reappraisal of the U.S. involvement in Europe could trigger a generalized *sauve qui peut* whereby the nationalisms of Europe would be unleashed with various bilateral deals within Europe, including Germany looking to the East, initially with France but ultimately alone. Thus, a Franco-German *ménage à trois* with Moscow, staged mainly by Germany, would balance an Anglo-Saxon *pas de deux* choreographed by the United States. Depending on the goals these bilateral initiatives might seek for Europe, not to mention other deals struck between European states and non-European rogue regimes like Iraq, vital U.S. economic and strategic interests might be progressively at risk.

With the end of the Cold War transition, the U.S. leadership is questioned more openly in much of Europe, and by many of the European states. Still, even as it is questioned, it is not truly in question, whether in Europe or in the United States. Such broad acceptance of the desirability of a U.S. role in Europe matters. On both sides of the Atlantic, the case for American involvement is based on interests: nowhere else can there be found a relationship that is as *complete* as the relationship between North America (the

United States but also Canada) and Europe, a relationship that relies on decisive security ties, as well as on inescapable economic, political, and even cultural bonds.

There are many remaining points for derailment, however. In the coming years, causes for concern might include a Western defeat in the Balkans, meaning an unlikely decision to withdraw U.S. forces before the 1995 Dayton agreements are convincingly fulfilled, or without preserving minimal order in Kosovo. Derailment might also result from an unmanaged conflict in the Gulf or in the Middle East, which would reinforce a European perception that U.S. policies respond to national goals at the expense of the allies' needs, combined with a U.S. perception of the allies as fair-weather friends only. Derailment could also be caused by a military conflict in Asia, which the Europeans would choose to ignore because it would be viewed as an American-made issue (in Korea and over Taiwan) or because the sheer dimension of the conflict would be an invitation to ignore it (in the Indian subcontinent).

No less significantly, points of transatlantic derailment might also include an economic crisis reminiscent of the interwar years that bridged the gap between the two world wars. For example, a monetary storm in Europe after the launch of the euro—with, without, or because of an economic meltdown in Asia—could trigger an agonizing reappraisal of the post–Cold War transatlantic economic ties, notwithstanding the interests that justify these ties. Finally, a breakdown of the transatlantic ties could also result from a political crisis caused by an open conflict over burden sharing in Russia, or from an open confrontation over competing corporate interests in Asia or the Middle East. Such a crisis would lead the U.S. Congress to force unilateral actions by the U.S. executive branch, thereby sparking a counteraction by the EU Commission prompted by some of its members.

Thus, the main security challenges in Europe are mostly of Europe's own making. Whether with 16 or 19 members, NATO does not directly address many or most of these instabilities, except for the fact that it represents the conduit for a U.S. commitment that Europe continues to need because of its own insufficiencies, and continues to expect in spite of itself.

That NATO might stand at the margin of the most direct challenges to Europe's stability during the coming years is admittedly troubling. Yet, in 1949, too, the North Atlantic Treaty signed by the United States and 10 European states plus Canada did not address many of the most immediate security issues faced by the European allies, including imperial wars in the South and domestic political wars that, in some cases, came dangerously close to outright civil wars. After the Cold War, the commitment to NATO enlargement was made without explaining fully the interests that would justify it. Needless to say, it should have been the other way around: interests define commitments, and the will for a commitment emerges out of a shared awareness of the interests that justify that commitment.

After 1999, the case for enlarging NATO beyond 19 members should be made on strategic as well as institutional grounds. In other words, it will be necessary to define the alliance's needs for the missions and objectives sought by its 19 members, and it will be necessary, too, to determine which new members should be welcomed by either institution to fill the new political and security gaps opened by the ongoing rearticulation of Europe's civil and stable space.

Within that space, NATO and the EU are pursuing parallel paths of post–Cold War enlargement and reform, although the EU's greater collective awareness of what it must do is not matched by NATO's greater collective ability to act. For both institutions, the logic of enlargement and the modalities of reform have not been articulated. NATO enlargement has been mainly a policy without a rationale, notwithstanding the body of scholarly literature that helped promote it during the early post–Cold War years. Thus, in 1998, the decisive argument for enlargement was that the predictable cost of not enforcing the commitment to enlarge would outweigh the unpredictable costs of going ahead with a fairly prudent decision—prudent vis-à-vis the new members (limited in number and carefully selected as to their location) but also, therefore, vis-à-vis Russia. In other words, the justification for enlargement seemed to be that it was in the U.S. interest because it had been so declared. After enlargement to 19 was ratified by the U.S.

Senate, the decision to enlarge beyond 19, with or without a pause, should be based more explicitly on a strategic rationale.

Unlike NATO, the EU can justify its enlargement with an exclusively institutional argument because the EU has an identity of its own as, literally, the sixteenth member of the European Union. Affluence, and hence stability, in Europe is difficult to imagine without the EU. The same cannot be said of NATO, whose members would not necessarily lose their security without the guarantees offered by the Treaty and enforced by its organization. After 1999, the rationale for NATO enlargement will need to be more realistic, meaning that it should be threat-conscious in addition to being institution-conscious. No less important, the rationale will need to be made differently—depending on whether it is to apply to, say, Romania as compared to the Baltic states or one of the Balkan states. The security needs of each of these countries are bound to be different, as will their vulnerability to the evolution of Russian policies and objectives in the affected regions.

In 1949 as now, NATO and the first two enlargements that followed (in 1952 with Greece and Turkey, and in 1955 with the Federal Republic of Germany) provided a security context within which Europe's internal questions of political stability and economic growth could be addressed, and community building could be launched. NATO alone did not produce peace within the North Atlantic area, but the fact that it deterred war from without helped buy the time needed for reconstruction and reconciliation. This carries two implications. First, the European economic community was a by-product of, and a prerequisite for, the transatlantic security community. In other words, the idea of Europe and the Atlantic idea followed parallel tracks—each with its own locomotive, its own ambitions, its own capabilities—until such time as Europe would be so self-sufficient as to make the Atlantic idea redundant, or the American commitment would be so well rooted in reality as to make the idea of Europe secondary.

Accordingly, the evolution of NATO and the EU, including their enlargement as well as their institutional reforms, must now also be kept complementary. Questions of membership and interests—who and why, when and how?—are raised for a common Euro-Atlantic security space whose articulation began after the two world wars and proceeded during the Cold War. Each institution must remain aware of what the other does, as well as of what neither can do. NATO and EU members should be aware of countries that cannot soon enter either the EU or NATO, or both, whatever the reasons may be, and of countries that belong to only one of these institutions but not both, whether out of choice or of necessity.

Common Home

The integrated economic space of the European Union, in close association with the United States, and a common Euro-Atlantic security community explicitly based on U.S. power have already emerged. That space will be all the more cohesive and safe as it continues to respond to some of the features that helped define it over the past 50 years.

- First, the United States may not be a European Power, but it is a Great Power in Europe. To pretend the former is misleading. The very history of the United States makes the closeness of its relations with Europe still look somewhat unnatural. But the tangible components of the U.S. presence in Europe can no longer be ignored. Unlike the U.S. relationship with Asia, the U.S. relationship with Europe is complete.

- Second, the Atlantic Idea and the Idea of Europe are complementary. To pretend otherwise is self-defeating. After World War II, each was a precondition for the other. During the Cold War, each helped strengthen the other. After the Cold War, the future of each will condition that of the other.

- Third, NATO and its enlargement are only one institutional venue for a return of the East into the West as part of the rearticulation of space in Europe and across the Atlantic. To pretend otherwise is not only to reduce the totality of the Cold War legacies to one dimension, but also to distort that dimension.

- Fourth, the enlargement of the Western institutions is only beginning but it must remain finite. In other words, membership for all is not desirable for the good performance of either NATO or the EU or both, and membership in either the EU or NATO may not be desirable or beneficial for all states in Europe.

Integrating these features in the formulation of the questions and answers raised by the new security challenges Europe faces after the enlargement of NATO will help pursue the vision that was articulated 50 years ago as the Cold War was about to provide the rationale for a North Atlantic Treaty designed to extend America's stay in Europe. As these 50 years are remembered, they leave room for apprehension over what remains to be done, but even more convincingly, they provide much room, too, for considerable satisfaction over what has already been accomplished.

PART TWO

Half Past NATO,
Half Before Europe

4

The Logic of Dual Enlargement

A MONG THE MANY ISSUES THAT WILL DEFINE the terms of security in Europe early in the twenty-first century, few are as historically significant as the dual enlargement to the east of the North Atlantic Treaty Organization (NATO) and the European Union (EU). After 1945, the insanity of two world wars in slightly more than one generation created firm resolve in the United States and among some of the European states to make another major war in Europe unthinkable. To this effect, decisions involving the organization of a transatlantic security community with the United States and of a European economic community with Germany were linked. Under the protective umbrella of NATO guarantees that confirmed America's return to Europe, an ever more integrated civil space began to take form on the western part of the Continent. Expanding that space to the countries of Central and Eastern Europe (CCEE) now raises issues comparable to those faced after 1945: the reconstruction of states whose ideological captivity made them the prime European victims of the Cold War, and reconciliation with a defeated state, Russia, that must learn to live within the geographic boundaries imposed by the reality of its defeat.

In June 1993 the European Council summit meeting at Copenhagen decided that any country associated with the EU through "Europe Agreements" was to be eligible for the rights of membership as soon as it could satisfy the economic and political conditions required to assume the obligations of membership.[1] Five years later, in March 1998, half of the 10 CCEE applicants, plus Cyprus, began accession negotiations whose completion date was understandably kept unclear. Earlier, German chancellor Helmut Kohl and others, like French president Jacques Chirac, had periodically mentioned the year 2000 as the target date for EU enlargement. By early 1998, however, 2003 was widely viewed as a more realistic date, and some EU documents found it necessary to extend this "next period" of EU enlargement until the year 2006.[2]

These dates are less significant than the ways in which the substantive issues that condition membership are addressed during the intervening years. Such issues are all the more demanding because they are likely to force several agonizing adjustments for the EU's integrative effort as this effort has unfolded since the Rome Treaties were signed in 1957.

The first such issue is that given the high financial costs of enlargement, the commitment to maintain the EU budget at 1.27 percent of its members' Gross Domestic Product (GDP), or less, may force a significant overhaul of EU policies in several areas of primary concern to most CCEE states, including the Common Agricultural Policy (CAP) and the allocation of structural subsidies. In 1998, the four poorest EU states reached 74 percent of the average per capita income of all 15 members. For all 10 applicant countries, this average barely reached a third of the EU average. Under these conditions, enlargement would leave Greece as the only current member state eligible for support, and limits on available funds would probably force lower levels of EU support, relative to a member's gross domestic product (GDP), than has been received by Greece since it became a member in 1981.

Another issue is that with enlargement involving a large number of countries—probably no fewer, but possibly more, than 10—some anticipatory redesign of the EU structures will be necessary, including changes in voting procedures at the European Council, as well as the reorganization of an overburdened Commission and some rethinking of the role of the European Parliament. Moreover, the development of the European Central Bank (ECB) is likely to affect the distribution of power and influence within the EU (between the president of the Commission and the ECB president), as well as between the ECB president and the finance ministers of all member states.

In an implicit recognition of the failure of the Amsterdam Summit, the European Commission's *Agenda 2000* asked for another IGC "as soon as possible after 2000 to prepare the Union for enlargement by means of far-reaching reforms of the institutional provisions of [the Maastricht] Treaty." A central feature of the EU consensus in 1998, this call pointed to such a conference of the 15 member states by 2001 at the latest.

A third issue is that negotiations for EU enlargement are especially delicate because the perception of delayed membership, let alone the reality of nonmembership, for some states relative to their neighbors is probably more seriously damaging than delayed membership or nonmembership in NATO. The perverse effect of integration is that widening differences between members and nonmembers provides the ultimate evidence that the EU works. Since 1957, only Norway has deemed this evidence insufficient to justify membership (twice) after it had been negotiated successfully. In the East, the consequences of enlargement would be worsened if its pace were to be stalled after the first wave of new members creates enough disruptions to delay the next wave. In any case, as the terms of EU enlargement are defined, it can be assumed that foreign investments will be especially responsive to the most likely new members (within the Baltic region, for example). Open-ended delays could erode the political will for reforms in the neglected countries (like Romania), and some of the countries left out might look at their neighbors for different arrangements that would have significant security implications for the West (like Ukraine).

Another consideration is that every new EU member produces a different neighborhood that creates new demands and more expectations among non-EU countries, thus creating new responsibilities and more pressures on EU members and their institutions. Thus, it did not take long for Russia to state its own expectation after the European Commission took steps to begin negotiations with five states in the East, including, most pointedly, a former Soviet republic in the Baltic region. "In the near future," remarked the then-prime minister Victor Chernomyrdin in Brussels on July 18, 1997, "Russia should be in the EU."[3] EU membership for Russia, however, is no more likely than NATO membership, either in the near or the unpredictable future.[4] Yet, the EU cannot afford to neglect a state whose continued economic backwardness, let alone meltdown, would be of enormous significance to its neighbors in Europe and even, possibly, in Asia. Nor could the EU afford to ignore Ukraine after it has expanded to Poland, or Latvia and Lithuania after Estonia has been absorbed, or Slovakia after expansion to the Czech Republic and its other two neighbors in Central Europe, or other countries in Southeastern Europe after Slovenia has been welcomed.

As every stage of enlargement depends on the acceptance of specific terms and conditions by each EU country, *internal national* debates are as significant as the *intra-European* debate. In other words, the specific interests of each member state, and the perceptions of these interests by its partners, condition and ultimately produce the compromises and trade-offs over enlargement. With the erosion of the permissive consensus that characterized the rise of "Europe" after World War II, such internal debates can be increasingly influenced by changes in political leadership as statesmen who "won" the Cold War give way to political leaders whose emphasis is placed more narrowly on the need to win elections.

NATO enlargement is different—more demanding in some ways and less complex in others. It became the lead question of the post–Cold War order in Europe nearly as an afterthought—after, that is, the EU's display of its post-Maastricht institutional disarray and its post-Bosnia political impotence returned NATO to its natural condition of institutional primacy. Thus, the NATO decision to enlarge, in December 1995, came after the EU decision, in June 1993. This late start was due to the need for all 16 NATO members to agree on the necessity of enlargement (whether and why) before they could proceed (who and when)—a necessity that was not apparent in 1993, when the Clinton administration seemed more focused on Asia than it was on Europe, and Europe was more focused on the celebration of past gains than on the preparation of new tasks. For the EU, which was the institution first targeted for membership by countries in the East, the need for enlargement as a matter of principle was readily accepted—"a historic turnpoint for Europe . . . for the sake of [its] security, its economy, its culture, and its status in the world," declared Jacques Santer, the president of the European Commission, on July 16, 1997. Even after the decisions for both institutional enlargements had been made, however, the dynamics of each institution kept the process much slower for the EU than for NATO for several reasons:

- NATO is driven by one member state, the United States, without which the organization could not endure, while EU decisions on enlargement depend explicitly on the approval of all 15 members whose consent is required for every one of the 13 steps that define the process;

- the financial costs of EU enlargement cannot be as easily fudged or shared, and its political costs as easily managed or justified, as they are for NATO, both before and after accession has taken place;[5]

- the Washington Treaty, which was drafted in simple language, is flexible and relatively undemanding, whereas the Rome Treaties, written as a much more complex document, define an ever more rigorous discipline—a body of regulations and laws known as the *acquis communautaire*—that has become increasingly demanding for current members, let alone new ones.

Nor is this all. The different processes—directions and speeds—of both institutional enlargements have also had to respond to such considerations as

- NATO's need to take into account the strategic interests and political sensitivities of nonmembers (especially Russia but also Ukraine and the Baltic states), whereas the EU must accommodate the political preferences and economic apprehensions of its own members. The latter is a more difficult task, given the veto right of each EU state (which is more conclusive than the search for consensus that characterizes decisionmaking within NATO);

- a public indifference to NATO enlargement (but without any hostility toward NATO) as compared to a public ambivalence to the EU (which does not suggest indifference toward EU enlargement);[6]

- and for both NATO and the EU, the requirements of separate ratification debates that were and remain based on grounds of national interests ranked in terms of national priorities.

Finally, and most broadly, the processes of dual enlargement define the new forms of spatial differentiation that are replacing the system of territorial states in Europe.[7] In a post–Cold War environment of multiple allegiances, which can no longer be national only, inter-state relations are viewed increasingly through the prism of collective abstractions that are real so long as participating nation-states remain willing to accept the discipline of institutional membership as a matter of convenience because they can still ignore it as a matter of right.[8]

In both NATO and the EU, relations of complex interdependence that emerged in the Cold War have grown both more complex and more dependent. The complexity of these relations is extended by the proliferation of channels of communication between member states outside or within each institution, and between both institutions and nonmembers or other institutions. Relations between the United States and the EU, or between NATO and Russia, as distinct from bilateral relations between either the United States or Russia and EU or NATO members are examples of such complexity. So too are relations between NATO and the Western European Union (WEU) or the EU and the World Trade Organization (WTO). No less significant is an absence of alternative to institutional membership even for the largest states in each institution (including Germany in the EU and the United States in NATO), meaning a degree of dependence on making an initiative work if failure were to threaten the derailment of that institution. This condition was experienced during the debate on NATO enlargement to 19 members and the debate over Economic and Monetary Union (EMU).[9]

In earlier years, the state was fading as an economic actor. In more recent years, it has also been fading as a political and military actor—the former because of its growing submission to decisions made by institutional actors or some national actors within institutions, and the latter because of a widespread aversion to military power, which makes the use of force by one nation-state unlikely while keeping the use of force by many member states ever more difficult. These conditions prevail in the United States and the states of Europe, as well as among them, as part of a Euro-American relationship that is sufficiently intimate to define a common space across the Atlantic but remains insufficiently integrated to form a true community.

The Acquis Is the Key

After the Rome Treaties had been signed by a hard core of six European states in 1957, the size of "their" small community doubled as membership was extended to Denmark, Great Britain and Ireland in 1973, Greece in 1981, and Portugal and Spain in 1986. Revisions in institutional governance began with the Single European Act of 1987, also designed to prepare the then-European Community for the Single Market that was anticipated for 1992. By then, the fact of enlargement to 15 members that was decided at Maastricht in December 1991 demanded that additional treaty revisions be negotiated in a new IGC that was expected to conclude its work before the commitment to enlarge to the east could be enforced.[10] Convened in the spring of 1996, the IGC was to address such serious institutional issues as

- procedural reforms, like reviewing the range of issues open to qualified majority voting in the European Council, adopting superqualified or population-weighted majority voting that would protect and even strengthen the primacy of the larger members, and changing the presidency system in force for the European Council in order to ensure a rotation that would be less favorable to the smaller states; reviewing the role and power of the European Parliament (relative to the Commission and the Council, but also to national legislatures); and reappraising the composition of the European Commission (for example, reduce the number of commissioners to one or less per member state, depending on size and population, and change procedures for their nominations, including that of the Commission president);

- development of a Common Foreign and Security Policy (CFSP)—with more majority voting to define a unified EU policy, a single EU voice to present and defend that policy, and a stronger Western European Union (WEU) that could enforce that policy—in order to give Europe a regional military autonomy and global political influence commensurate with its economic weight and historic tradition;

- closer member state cooperation in the vital societal areas of justice and home affairs.

In Amsterdam in 1997, the IGC did not realize the high expectations it had raised the year before in Florence. At any rate, these were probably too high for a process of integration that is incremental and reactive by nature. To make matters worse, as the 15 member states prepared for the final weeks of negotiations in the spring of 1997, the political landscape in all three main EU states was dramatically changed with the suddenly fragile German government of Helmut Kohl, a newly assertive British government led by Tony Blair, and a newly elected government in France led by Lionel Jospin. Trade-offs that had concluded previous intergovernmental negotiations could no longer be developed either between France and Germany (and, therefore, between them and their partners) or, lacking a Franco-German consensus, by Britain with either France or Germany. As a result, there could be, and was, no change in most main issues involving the Commission, the Council, or the European Parliament. Nor could there be truly significant decisions with regard to CFSP, about which the long-awaited Mr. Europe remained mostly ignored even after he had been named.

In sum, the IGC that was expected to complete EU enlargement in the West (pending changes in countries that had declined membership, like Norway and Switzerland) and launch EU enlargement to the East proved to be a non-event. Its main contribution was to end, so the EU could formally begin negotiations with five CCEE countries (the same three countries picked by NATO plus Estonia and Slovenia) and with Cyprus. Yet, the same difficult questions of institutional governance remain: looming ahead, in or around the year 2001, is another IGC when the 15 EU members will have to make the decisions they failed to make in

1997 on their behalf as well as on behalf of upcoming new members.[11]

The debate over budget reform is also directly relevant to EU enlargement. The Commission's commitment to keeping the spending cap of 1.27 percent of GDP during the period 2000–2006, and Germany's growing determination to lower its contribution to that budget, could make the EU funds available for economic and social cohesion insufficient as, even under benign economic conditions, disparities among and within current members are expected to widen. When the EU was expanding in the West, new members were alternatively richer (in 1973, except for Ireland), then poorer (in 1981 and 1986), and then richer again (in 1995, with Austria, Norway, and Sweden). As the EU expands to the east, however, the CCEE applicants for membership, which will increase the EU population by one-third while increasing its GDP by one-twentieth only, are poised to absorb substantial amounts of aid for which all qualify in full. Predictably, poorer EU countries that rely on generous levels of EU aid are not prepared to accept more competition for such funds from new members, and their misgivings can be amply voiced during the negotiations leading to both the next IGC and the new enlargement.

The issue of budget reform is especially significant to member states that have large agricultural sectors—which is the case for most CCEE applicants where farmers who can produce plenty are prepared to sell cheap: altogether, these countries would double the EU's agricultural workforce and increase its cultivated surface area by more than 40 percent.[12] Because much of this area would come from countries north of the parallel on which the French city of Lyon is situated, relatively poorer EU countries in the south may be less directly affected than their partners in the north. For example, the loss of income to German farmers from enlargement has been estimated at as much as one-fifth of current revenues; to make matters politically worse among relevant constituencies, German financial contributions to EU agriculture would reportedly increase by about 10 percent over their 1997 level.

Although farmers in Southern Europe may be less affected by enlargement than their counterparts in northern countries, they join the debate over proposals initiated in Northern Europe to "renationalize" agricultural policy by making each EU country responsible for direct payments to their own farmers. Predictably, any such proposal is anathema for European governments that cannot support their farmers with the same largesse as the EU Commission. Thus, South European farmers who do not oppose eastward expansion on the basis of increased competition are still likely to oppose it for its impact on CAP and the reforms that CAP is likely to pursue in order to accommodate the costs of enlargement.

The difficulties raised by budgetary questions should not be exaggerated, however. Projections often tend to be too rigid. For example, the scarcity of financial resources does not account for the more robust growth that might follow the launching of the euro. Even without a measurable euro-boost, a modest economic expansion relative to earlier expectations could still reduce the EU budget relative to GDP for the last two years of the 1990s, with such decline expected to continue in subsequent years and after enlargement. Estimated budget savings would cover a large share of the projected outlays for enlargement.[13]

Nor is spending for current and new members likely to remain fixed. Projections of future needs for structural funds are not reliable measures of the EU's pre-accession aid strategy, which might stimulate growth among applicants before membership is granted, or for the imposition of lower ceilings (relative to GDP) on the aid provided by the EU for any one of its members. Agricultural projections are also affected by the disproportionate weight of Poland relative to other applicants: not only do farms in Poland represent nearly 30 percent of all current EU farms, they are all small and few of them are reportedly viable. Because economic growth in the CCEE countries would reduce their need for EU resources generally, as was the case with other initially "poor" members like Ireland, it would also increase their internal demand for foodstuffs: together with a growing worldwide demand, the new EU members could, therefore, help firm up prices, reduce the overall levels of subsidies, and mitigate the impact of CAP reforms.

While the 15 EU members struggle to preserve their *acquis* by defraying or delaying the financial costs of enlargement, the CCEE applicants must prepare their own constituencies for the political and societal costs of enforcing the 1,400-odd items of key EU market legislation. A moving target that grows continuously, this *acquis* is made more difficult as it penetrates the most sensitive areas of national sovereignty: the protection of borders and population flows, with the rigid demands of the Schengen agreements; the surrender of national currencies to the euro and the discipline of the European Central Bank; and even, hypothetically, an erosion of national autonomy in foreign and security policy with new EU decisions involving CFSP and WEU.

Dual Enlargement

Both NATO and the EU are the flagships of the institution-based European structure developed by the United States over a 12-year period after 1945. These policies were shaped by interests—economic, political, and strategic—that grew during the Cold War. The totality of these interests is not matched anywhere else outside the Western Hemisphere. What the states of Europe do and fail to do, as sovereign nation-states but also as members of the EU, has direct, and often vital, consequences for the United States. The risks to U.S. leadership and influence raised by a more united and stronger Europe, with a currency and even (ultimately) an army of its own, are prospective and hypothetical; the risks to U.S. interests and ideals raised by a weak and divided Europe are immediate and tangible. In other words, the gravest risks raised by "Europe" to the United States are risks of institutional setbacks and failure rather than risks of institutional advances. What initiatives the EU launches, and how these are pursued, is not a U.S. responsibility. The United States is a power in Europe—arguably the only active Great Power on the Continent—but it is not a European power.[14] Nonetheless, the EU is a very important U.S. interest because of what it means for stability and affluence in Europe, where the United States does have vital economic and geopolitical interests.

Thus, although decisions affecting either Western institution can be separated, the two processes of NATO and EU enlargement remain inseparable. Moving at different speeds, responding to different needs and different priorities, and aiming at different goals and different aspirations, these two institutional processes move on parallel tracks, as they did during the Cold War, notwithstanding a lingering temptation to envision "Europe" as an alternative to NATO and an escape from U.S. leadership. In short, the enlargement of the EU and the enlargement of NATO complete each other because each institution provides a dimension (security or economic) that the other cannot be expected to cover as fully, and even an identity (European or Atlantic) without which the other cannot be sufficient.

This is not meant to imply that the EU does not have a security role to play, or that NATO does not have a political role as well. In effect, reconciliation between France and Germany took place in the context of the EU more than it did within NATO, which was unable to provide for reconciliation between the two countries, Greece and Turkey, that were included for the first NATO enlargement in 1953. Yet, on the whole, for any institutional orphan in Eastern Europe, defense is a matter that is best left to NATO, prosperity is an aspiration that is best left to the EU, and stability is a necessity that can best result from both institutions.

The enlargement of the EU and of NATO also complete each other because membership in either institution (gained in its own right) can help compensate for nonmembership in the other (denied for reasons of its own), as was the case for Turkey throughout the Cold War. Thus, European countries that belong to one of these institutions only are natural candidates for membership in the other, and countries that remain ineligible for membership for one of these institutions should be priority contenders for the other. The EU neutral states that have stayed out of NATO are examples of the former condition, as is Turkey, a NATO country that remains excluded from the EU in spite of its repeated efforts to join it. Romania and Bulgaria are examples of the latter condition, as countries that can satisfy the NATO criteria but are unlikely to meet the criteria for EU membership for many years to come.

Finally, enlargements of the EU and NATO complete each other because the transparency of the national debates over EU and NATO enlargements influences subsequent national debates over the role of the United States in Europe and the future of the European states in the EU. Thus, failure to enlarge the EU promptly could have ramifications for NATO enlargement after 1999 as opponents to the latter would rely on the slow pace of the former to justify their position. Similarly, more U.S. calls for a larger European share of the financial costs of NATO enlargement to 19 could cause more debate in Europe over the costs of EU enlargement to the east. Finally, in either case, more public debate over the merits of enlargement can renew a public debate over the merits of the institution itself.

In the United States, the EU has been second in importance to NATO. When the EU has moved center stage, it has usually been viewed as a competitor for regional leadership and a rival on global trade issues. In short, U.S. perceptions of the EU are often ambivalent because U.S.-EU relations are often adversarial, including the need to sustain leadership on the American side and a determination to provide a shield against it on the European side. Examples of such ambivalence as a matter of perceptions, and of transatlantic discord as a matter of fact, abound.[15] In post–Cold War years, this discord has become ever more sensitive to domestic pressures that make the tone of recurring disputes more bitter, and their resolution more difficult.

Early in the Clinton administration, and sometime after the Maastricht Treaty had been signed and the single market launched, many in the United States accepted Europe's contention that its time was about to come—for the better, at last, or for the worse, alas. Whether in the context of the political and economic goals set at Maastricht in 1991, or in the context of security priorities set in Bosnia and beyond Europe, this assumption remained unmet. In 1995, therefore, the post–Cold War discourse over Europe and its future gave way to a debate over NATO and its future. This outcome was a European failing as much as, or more than, it was an actual American choice.

Initial decisions about NATO's enlargement were executive agreements negotiated and signed by the heads of state or government of all 16 members:

- to organize a cooperative relationship with Russia (and also Ukraine) before and beyond a first wave of enlargement that was designed to accommodate its most immediate concerns;

- to upgrade the NATO "partners" into nonmember members of the Alliance, with appropriate room for consultation before decisions are made and with effective measures for active contributions after these decisions are enforced;

- to reassert the cohesion of NATO at 16 by seeking a final settlement of France's return as a full member of NATO prior to NATO's formal enlargement to 19 members, which was known to be scheduled for April 1999;

- and, after April 1999, to initiate (or at least consider) accession talks with other applicants for NATO membership whose identity, however, would not have to be revealed immediately.

For the most part, the decisions over NATO enlargement (who and when) were never in doubt, unlike the final outcomes of the IGC negotiations viewed as a parallel prelude to EU enlargement (when and who). The NATO decisions had been made, at least implicitly, and could be anticipated, even explicitly, long before the Madrid Summit was arranged, let alone held—and long before they were formally announced, let alone confirmed.[16] From the moment enlargement began to enter the public debate, in early 1995, the states of Central Europe were the only credible candidates for quick admission, and the exclusion of Slovakia was made on political grounds. It was deceptive for the United States to pretend that other countries were in contention, and it was self-deceptive for the Europeans to believe otherwise. Yet, the process of NATO enlargement would have been smoother had consultation with the allies and public deliberation on both sides of the Atlantic been more explicit earlier.

By early 1997, the United States was the only country with the ability to stand in the way of NATO's enlargement to 19 members. Other NATO members, let alone Russia, could neither prevent nor modify it. Before Madrid, enlargement would have proceeded even if Russia had rejected the NATO offer for a separate agreement. Yet, the U.S. ability to produce such an agreement in late May 1997 helped moderate the national debates over enlargement in the

United States and all other NATO countries. At Madrid, European vocal preferences for more new members did not affect the summit meeting and its outcome either, and even France's decision to delay its return to an organization it should not have left in the first place proved of little significance. After Madrid, the NATO calculation of costs responded to political imperatives in the United States more than to security imperatives in Europe and for the projected new members.

In short, the debate over NATO enlargement confirmed the distinctiveness of NATO relative to the EU. In the end, NATO is an organization at (1+15) because one state, the United States, can impose its will on the other 15 members. In contrast, the EU is an institution at (15-1) because any one member can frustrate the will of all its partners in the community.

In recent years, the NATO calendar has responded to arbitrary deadlines set by a cumbersome agenda of bilateral summits and multilateral NATO, EU, and U.S.-EU meetings. The rigidity of the calendar has been worsened by a history that has imposed its memories of past events to order decisions for the future. Thus, the fiftieth anniversary of the June 1947 Marshall Plan appeared early as an irresistible target date for a formal announcement on enlargement, at a NATO Summit in Madrid in July 1997. Subsequently, the April 1999 Washington Summit was to parallel the Washington Treaty of April 1949. The importance of such a rigid calendar is real. Each deadline forces new decisions, and each decision is the source of new deadlines, but failure to enforce any decision endangers the next deadline and can force a reappraisal of earlier decisions. In the spring of 1998, the coincidental overlap between the debates on NATO enlargement and U.S. troop deployment in Bosnia made the NATO decision dependent on the planned U.S. departure from Bosnia by June 1, 1998. If confirmed, such a decision would have compromised the Dayton accords, but it would also have disrupted significantly the national debates for the ratification of NATO enlargement, in the U.S. Senate as well as in several NATO countries. Accordingly, President Clinton's early announcement, in December 1997, that U.S. forces would stay indefinitely aimed at preserving NATO no less than at sustaining Bosnia.

Enlarging NATO from 16 to 19 members met the expectations of a few Eastern countries concerned over the role of Russia in post–Cold War Europe, but it also met the concerns of even more countries in the West that did not know what to expect about the U.S. role. Failure to enlarge would have compromised NATO's future, and, by implication, the future of the United States in Europe. Only after the magnitude of the vote for ratification in the U.S. Senate had served as a demonstration of its commitment to maintaining a central role on the Continent could the national debates on NATO and its enlargement start on their own merits: first, with a review of unresolved questions of NATO missions, capabilities, and leadership, and next with a discussion of further enlargement, if any, after 1999.

In the short term, such internal debates could still be influenced by many external issues. One of these would be a botched withdrawal of U.S. forces in Bosnia because of, or prior to, a concerted attempt to enforce the Dayton accords in full (including the arrest and punishment of war criminals)—which would be the first withdrawal of U.S. military forces from Europe before the war has been ended and won. The evidence of American failures in Bosnia or elsewhere in the Balkans (including Kosovo), would end the public permissiveness for U.S. activism in Europe and transform the general tone of transatlantic relations. Such failures would be especially significant if they included U.S. casualties suffered on behalf of commitments that few Americans know or care to understand.

Another critical external issue would be a crisis in or with Turkey, whose European neighbors are bitterly resented for their politico-cultural hostility over the central issues of EU membership and Cyprus. Even as the Clinton administration aims its criticism at the European states for failing to respond to Turkey's bid for EU membership, the United States, too, shares a broad Western attitude of neglect: U.S. security assistance to Turkey declined from $500 million in grants in 1991 to $175 million in market rate loans in 1997. Meanwhile, U.S. forces have declined from more than 20,000 personnel and dependents at 20 installations to less than 8,000 personnel at six installations.[17]

Yet another external issue would be an ill-defined drama in Moscow, before or with the next presidential elections scheduled for the year 2000, and resulting from a new political leadership that would reappraise post–Cold War policies and attitudes in the midst of an economic and societal meltdown of the country; and, similarly, ill-defined dramas between Russia and any one of the former Soviet republics, because or in spite of Russian intentions and ambitions. Neither NATO nor even EU enlargement affect internal conditions in Russia, but the internal evolution of Russia inevitably has an impact on NATO and the EU. While postwar Russia has hardly shown the dynamism of the Federal Republic of Germany after World War II, it has not yet shown the disarray of the Weimar Republic after World War I. In short, problems in Russia are Europe's problem, although Europe's problems are not Russia's problem.

External issues could also include a new armed conflict in the Middle East, which would confirm Europe's sense of a failed U.S. leadership, or other rounds of inconclusive military confrontation with Iraq, which would confirm America's view of countries in Europe as unreliable allies whose support can be expected only after success has become evident. Wars in the Middle East have been fraught with consequences for Europe: a change of government in Britain and the fall of the Fourth Republic in France in the wake of the 1956 Suez crisis, stormy monetary turbulence after the 1967 war (which ultimately prompted an attempt at economic and monetary union at the 1969 Hague Summit), a sweep of political majorities in the main European countries after the first oil crisis in 1973–74, and a repeat performance after the second oil crisis in 1979–81, and even the spillover of the 1990–91 Gulf war as a catalyst for the Algerian crisis and its spillover in Southern Europe. In 1999, another such crisis would be all the more significant as it would coincide with the launching of the euro, when every lost percentage point of economic growth in Europe can threaten the EU's ambitious timetable.

Enlargement of NATO to 19 members hardly ends the debate over NATO and its future. Thus, after 1999 the door could be left open for an undetermined number of new members in

Southeastern Europe (including Slovenia, Romania, and Bulgaria), Central Europe (Slovakia), and some former Soviet republics, including all three Baltic states (gradually or collectively) and even Ukraine. Beginning soon after 1999 and extending for many years, such further NATO enlargement would take place on security grounds, without but not against Russia, whose benign consent would continue to be managed through the Founding Act signed before the 1997 summit in Madrid. Membership in NATO could also be extended on grounds of regional stability, within and even beyond each applicant country, in the absence of an institutional alternative that would permit that country to pursue economic and political reform in the name of its ongoing integration in the West.

Alternatively, enlargement to 19 could close the door, however temporarily, on any new member. During such a pause, the desirability of any future enlargement would be decided on the basis of NATO's ability to absorb the initial wave of three new members, as well as on security needs, in and beyond Europe. The need and duration of such a pause would also result from developments in Russia, before and after the next presidential election. Finally, given the lack of a firm NATO consensus over the selection of new members, and given, too, the potential of a reinforced Partnership for Peace program as an alternative to NATO membership, an open-ended pause would provide a time-out before decisions that might prove divisive and even dangerous for Europe and its relations with the United States.

In Europe meanwhile, launching the euro in January 1999 will not end the debate over EMU any more than enlarging NATO to 19 ends the debate over NATO. The difference between EMU and NATO enlargement is hardly negligible, however. After 1999, NATO and its members can live with a pause before any additional enlargement. With regard to the euro, neither the EU nor its members would be able to endure readily the turbulence caused by an inability to proceed on schedule. This is the end game: a triumphant euro would define the "ever closer union" envisioned by the Rome Treaties, while its collapse would risk bringing the EU to a halt without the *relance* that has usually accompanied institutional setbacks in the past.

As was the case with the European Monetary System (EMS) for several years after its establishment in 1979, the EMU debate will continue in the streets and in the marketplace for several years: unlike what John Maynard Keynes liked to say, the euro faces better prospects for life in the long term than in the short term. After 1999, evidence of success will be needed quickly by each euro state to rebuild public confidence in the EU as a provider of affluence rather than a consumer of the state's providence. Such evidence would take the form of job creation, measured mainly in terms of a steady decline in unemployment rates. Otherwise, a deepening sense of failure would raise new obstacles for the completion of the reform-minded IGC and new delays for eastward enlargement.

In short, the euro is Europe's "question of destiny"[18]—the ultimate test of Europe's political will to move into and through the twenty-first century as a union of states. A weak and erratic euro that would fail to become the sole legal tender for all EU countries by 2002, as scheduled, would damage Europe's and America's confidence in the EU. Less confidence in the EU would increase Europe's dependence on NATO (and, by implication, U.S. leadership), but it might also make Americans lose confidence in both the EU for what it could not do and NATO for what it would still have to do (including enlargement in each case).

After years of making a euro-boost the justification of euro-wide austerity, an erratic performance of the euro would be potentially disastrous, causing not only turbulence in the marketplace, but also anger in the streets. From one election to the next, Euroskepticism might rise as a winning political issue, a condition that young political leaders who have made winning elections their main conviction would not ignore for long. As the debate would go back and forth, from the streets to the marketplace and from the national capitals to the European Commission in Brussels and the ECB in Frankfurt, calls for withdrawal from EMU before 2002 would rise irrespective of their consequences. Such calls might not be heard at first, but they would raise new questions about the EU and its impact on economic affluence and political stability. As a result, IGC-2001 would be stalled. Without the required institutional changes, but also without the robust economies needed to pay for enlargement, accession negotiations would also be stalled. Such disarray within the EU would affect the United States, whose wariness with Europe would spill over into its willingness to enlarge NATO further—to the satisfaction of Russia, whose new president, elected in 2000, could redouble his pressures for a more forceful Russian role in Europe and at its periphery.

Admittedly, a triumphant euro will force new challenges and many adjustments on U.S. policymakers: making this extraordinary initiative work will give the EU a confidence that might complicate the exercise of U.S. leadership in NATO. Yet, granted that what is good for Europe is not always equally good for the United States, what is bad for Europe almost always proves to be just as bad for the United States. Historically, America has suffered most when Europe started something it could not complete on its own—be it a revolution whose aspirations were more admirable than its execution, a war whose logic was in doubt even before it escalated into slaughter, or, now, a single currency over which it seems willing to gamble its future because it may not have enough of a future otherwise. In many EU countries, what has been accomplished to start the euro has transformed the boundaries of what used to be viewed as politically possible. Beyond these boundaries there is now an open frontier that will define not only the new Europe but also the modalities of its relations with the United States.

Old World Renewed

Decisions by and about the EU, and decisions by and about NATO, come together. Neither institution can ignore the interests and aspirations of countries that respond to the criteria for membership. Nor can either institution be indifferent to the implications which membership in one of them has on the other and its members. NATO enlargement widens a North Atlantic area of security that is guaranteed by American power, EU enlargement widens a European community of prosperity that benefits American interests, and both widen the boundaries of stability in the West to the advantage of all. These institutional processes of enlargement are welcomed by countries in the East, but they are driven by countries in the West that need to complete the institutional structure they started after World War II.

That NATO would have expanded to the east before the EU is not surprising. A failure of U.S. will over NATO ratification after enlargement had been formally announced by all 16 NATO members would have been comparable to the refusal to ratify membership in the League of Nations after its covenant had been negotiated by U.S. president Woodrow Wilson as part of the overall settlement that ended World War I (and set the stage for World War II). Because such a failure would have raised unprecedented doubts about the reliability of the North Atlantic Treaty, it would have eroded the credibility of NATO, which is the institution of choice for the protection of U.S. interests in Europe.

An especially surprising feature of the pre-1999 debate on enlargement is how little impact it had on public perceptions and preferences on either side of the Atlantic. Opposition remained the privilege of an intellectual elite, but the general public accepted enlargement as a fait accompli that did not seem to be of great significance. After 1999, however, the process of NATO enlargement beyond 19 members is open to a much more serious debate because

- membership of the Baltic states will be sought and even expected, either on their own terms or as part of multiple trade-offs in the United States and between all NATO states that sponsor membership of other countries in the Balkans (especially Romania and Slovenia) and elsewhere (including Ukraine);

- an attempt at including former Soviet republics in NATO would harden Russia's opposition to enlargement, and make it more convincing than was the case when enlargement was limited to Poland and its neighbors in Central Europe. Such opposition not only could damage the course of Western relations with Russia, but it could also influence Moscow's relations with its neighbors and even political conditions in Russia; and

- in the United States as well as in Europe, objections to further enlargement to other countries in Eastern Europe are likely to be raised early and before the commitment is made, despite the forceful public pressures exerted by the prospective new members.

For all these reasons, the Madrid decisions of July 1997 should not be construed as a firm U.S. and NATO commitment for an immediate expansion to other countries in the East as a means to reward patience and alleviate their insecurities. The commitments made in Madrid by all 16 NATO members were not designed to be a blank check for an open-ended enlargement of their organization. As stated by President Clinton at the close of the summit, additional countries will become NATO members "when they are ready and the time is right," which suggested not only that they were not ready yet, but also that they could be ready at a time that may not be right, from the standpoint of the organization as well as of its members—and, alternatively, that the time for further enlargement might be right before applicants were actually ready. Indeed, these criteria were spelled out in the final Madrid communiqué, which explicitly envisioned the next decisions for enlargement as "serv[ing] the overall political and strategic interest of the alliance" (including, but not limited to, the United States) and "overall European security and stability" (including consideration of Russia and its interests).

Although other countries in the East will eventually join NATO, the enlargement of the Western security community is likely to face some delay whose consequences will be less disruptive if this de facto pause is used to fill the gaps between both institutions. After 1999, a NATO at 19 that would await EU enlargement could still pursue an enlargement of its own to some of the neutral states of the Cold War, including Austria, but also, over time, Finland and Sweden, and even Ireland. Such a constructive pause would give both Western institutions an increasingly similar security space. It would also prevent backdoor security commitments made on behalf of EU states whose membership in the WEU gives them indirect access to the NATO guarantees before they gain NATO membership.

A parallel logic applies to EU enlargement. Admittedly, beyond 1999 the EU will face many urgent priorities as its members put their domestic houses in order while they strive to make the euro work as a strong and stable global currency, and as they revise their rules of governance before they deepen and widen their institutions further. Although EU enlargement cannot be expected too soon, protracted delays would threaten a new division of Europe, first along economic lines but soon along political and security lines as the consequences of a growing economic gap between EU and non-EU states would discourage democratic reforms and encourage new and closer relations among non-EU (and non-NATO) states led by Russia. These new divisions in Europe would be especially significant because EU failure to enlarge would also raise doubts in the United States over the EU's reliability as a provider of stability in post–Cold War Europe.

Thus, the dilemma of EU enlargement is that it must simultaneously act swiftly to calm the skeptics across the Atlantic, and avoid disrupting the NATO process, and take its time to make sure that current and new members alike are ready to face the economic costs and political consequences of enlargement. Such a dilemma could be best resolved with a gradual expansion of EU membership whereby the earlier admission of smaller applicants first (like Slovenia and Estonia) would help gain the time needed to negotiate the more demanding admission of the larger states in Central Europe. In addition, a gradual convergence of European membership in NATO and the EU, based on decisions made separately by their members, would make it possible for each institution to take its time when preparing for the next round of enlargement—as the EU did while waiting for NATO before 1997, and as NATO could now do while waiting for the EU after 1999.

The new members selected by both NATO and the EU have responded to this logic, as a matter of fact if not as a deliberate choice. From the start of the post–Cold War era, no enlargement of either Western institution was conceivable without Poland, but for NATO especially to expand only to Poland would have revived many historic fears among its neighbors, including Russia. After NATO had confirmed its choice of new members in Central Europe (without the Slovak Republic), the EU's designated new members included the NATO candidates, as well as countries from the two main regions neglected by NATO, namely, the Balkans and the Baltics.

Such mutually complementary approaches to enlargement require two qualifications, however. First, regional clusters of states should be respected; if not, completion of the cluster should be achieved as soon as criteria for membership are met, be it Central Europe for NATO or the Baltic states for the EU (but not the Balkans for either organization because of the unsettled conditions in the former Yugoslavia). Second, no country in any region should be allowed to remain an institutional orphan for too long. This condition is especially true for Romania, which is unlikely to qualify for EU membership for many years after it will have been explicitly recognized as qualified for NATO membership. Thus, beginning with the Madrid NATO Summit in July 1997 and the EU London Summit in March 1998, and extending until the years beyond the fiftieth anniversary of the Rome Treaties in 2007, NATO and EU enlargement might proceed as shown in the figure opposite.

Such juxtaposition of NATO and the EU will face many critics. In the United States, Europe is often viewed as a tiresome and hopeless consumer of American time and assets: it is still the Old World. The EU, meanwhile, is dismissed as a failure and its members as relics of the past—including a cultural identity that no longer matches the new demographic trends in the United States. In short, America's future is said to be elsewhere, in Asia mostly but also, to an extent, in the Western Hemisphere.

In Europe, too, U.S. leadership is often viewed as an intrusive and deceptive producer of visions that expects excessive contributions from its allies' scarce resources and can occasionally add recklessly to the security risks they face in their immediate regional neighborhoods. According to many in Europe, an especially appealing feature of the euro is that it will provide the European states with the tools needed to challenge the American hegemony, economically but politically as well.

Finally, within Europe, a Union that was welcomed during the Cold War as a shield against U.S. power and an alternative to a history of permanent conflicts and periodic wars is now questioned

NATO and EU Enlargement:
Converging Parallelism

NATO, Madrid (July) At 16	**1997**	
NATO RATIFICATION	**1998**	**EU,** London (March) At 15
At 19 Czech Republic, Hungary, Poland	**1999**	EURO LAUNCH
At 19 + Neutrals Austria; Finland, Sweden; Ireland Orphans Romania, Bulgaria	**2000**	At 15 + 1 + 1 Slovenia, Estonia
	2003	
At many New EU members Slovenia, Estonia Geographic Clusters Slovakia, Latvia/ Lithuania		+ 3 Czech Republic, Hungary, Poland + 1 + 1 Malta, Cyprus + . . . Norway
	2007	**U.S.-EU TREATY**
		At many Romania; Bulgaria . . . Turkey
. . . .	**2010**	. . . .

Overlapping NATO/EU Membership

for being too unwieldy, illegitimate, and painful: unwieldy because of a bureaucracy that erodes the sovereignty and the identity of its members, illegitimate because this bureaucracy lacks democratic credentials and transparency, and painful because its action is now viewed as a consumer of affluence and a producer of hardship.

Such doubts over the decisions that loom ahead reflect too much ambivalence over the accomplishments that lie behind. By the standards of history no less than by the standards of self-interest, U.S. policies toward Europe, including their emphasis on the construction of a strong and united Europe, have been extraordinarily successful. They have served America well, and they have served the nations of Europe well too. Enlarging NATO raises many risks, some political and others military, and enlarging the EU presents many costs, some financial and others societal. Yet, far worse would be the risks and the costs of nonenlargement—stemming from a refusal to pursue enlargement after it was sought, to impose a pause after it has been decided, and to enforce the decision after it has been announced.

National confusion in the United States over NATO enlargement (and to an extent NATO itself) and in Europe over the future of the EU (and to an extent the EU as well) does not result from the fact that there is no case to be made based on established interests and possible alternatives. More simply, the case has not been made yet, thereby enabling critics to be heard irrespective of their arguments or intentions. The U.S. case is about the interest of the United States in attending to a common Euro-Atlantic space whose significance is too vital to be left to the inflated ambitions of some European states or to the care of European institutions that are still in the making. As for the EU, the case will be made more forcefully when pandering majorities in Europe stop pretending that every difficult step taken by their governments responds to the dispassionate whims of Brussels rather than to the harsh social, political, and economic realities uncovered in each national capital.

In sum, in every EU member state that is also a member of NATO, as well as for all NATO members that do not belong to the EU, the cost of action may seem high but the cost of inaction would be much higher. This, perhaps, is the most enduring legacy of the Cold War: that the institutions inherited from 50 years of

East-West conflict over Europe would now be used to bid farewell to the instabilities inherited from 500 years of wars in Europe.

Notes

1. John Van Oudenaren, "Poland's Accession to the European Union: Outlook and Options" (CSIS Occasional Papers in European Studies, OR-96/14, August 1996), 10. Note, however, the emphasis placed in Copenhagen on "the Union's capacity to absorb new members, while maintaining the momentum of European integration." Such restrictive criteria of inclusion, also adopted for NATO enlargement, can stall enlargement on grounds that the institution is not ready.

2. "Agenda 2000: For a Stronger and Wider Europe," European Commission, Press Release IP/97/660, Doc. 97/9, Strasbourg/Brussels, 16 July 1997.

3. The EU is already Russia's largest trading partner, accounting for two-fifths of its foreign trade in 1993. EU-Russia Relations, MEMO 97/22, February 28, 1997.

4. "I see no prospects for Russia joining the European Union," acknowledged Foreign Minister Igor Ivanov while meeting EU officials in Vienna. "Our country is simply too large, the scale of Russia is too grandiose." Reuters wire, October, 1998.

5. The costs of NATO enlargement are a matter of assumptions, and these assumptions can vary enough to explain the considerable cost variations that have emerged over the past few years. See for example, Ronald D. Asmus, Richard Kugler, and Steve Larrabee, "What Will NATO Enlargement Cost," *Survival* 38, no. 3 (Autumn 1996).

6. Between 1993 and 1996, surveys consistently confirmed widespread public support for NATO in Europe—83 percent in Britain, 81 percent in Germany, and 76 percent in France (in 1996). Support for NATO has also remained strong in the United States, in the 75 percent range. Perceptions in Europe that a European defense force can replace NATO are not widespread—9 percent in Germany, 16 percent in Italy, and 18 percent in Britain and France. *The New European Security Architecture: Volume II*, USIA Office of Research and Media Reaction (September 1996). Also, Steven Kull, *Americans on Expanding NATO: A Study of US Public Attitudes*, Program on International Policy Attitudes, Center for International and Security Studies at Maryland (CISSM), February 13, 1997. In 1997, prior to signing an agreement with Russia, public support fell to 42 percent in Britain and 38 percent in Germany—which suggests that post–1999 NATO enlargement to the former Soviet republics could be directly influenced by Moscow. *Opinion Analysis*, USIA, Office of Research and Media Reaction, M-27-97 (February

7, 1997). By comparison, more than three out of five Europeans (61 percent) believed that EU enlargement would be a "good thing," but slightly more than one out of two viewed the EU similarly by the close of 1996 (55 percent, an all-time low). *Together in Europe*, EU Newsletter for Central Europe, no. 176, April 1, 1997. Also, *How much popular support is there for the EU*, Philip Morris Institute Paper, April 1997, vol. 12, p. 44. Some polls even suggest that the view of the EU is more positive in the United States than in Europe. Steven Kull, *Seeking a New Balance, A Study of American and European Public Attitudes on Transatlantic Issues* (CISSM, June 1998), p. 19.

7. John Ruggie, "Territoriality and beyond: problemizing modernity in international relations," *International Organization* (Winter 1993): 149–174. Also, John Herz, "Rise and Demise of the Territorial State," *World Politics* (July 1957): 473–493.

8. Ernst Haas, *Beyond the Nation State* (Stanford: Stanford University Press, 1964), 51.

9. In the early 1970s, Robert Keohane and Joseph Nye identified "complex interdependence" as the availability of multiple channels for connecting the units, the absence of hierarchy among issues (i.e., the non-primacy of military security issues over the agenda), and the continued (although lesser) role of military force when dealing with governments outside the region. These conditions, which had barely begun to emerge when Professors Keohane and Nye were writing their seminal work, now characterize the EU. Robert Keohane and Joseph Nye, *Power and Interdependence: World Politics in Transition* (Boston: Little Brown, 1977).

10. For example, David Cameron, "The 1992 Initiative," in Alberta M. Sbragia, ed., *Euro-Politics: Institutions and Policymaking in the "New" European Community* (Washington, DC: Brookings Institution, 1992). Also, Stephan Haggard et al., "Integrating the Two Halves of Europe: Theories of Interests, Bargaining and Institutions," in Robert O. Keohane, S. Hoffmann, and J. Nye, eds., *After the Cold War: International Institutions in Europe* (Cambridge: Harvard University Press, 1993).

11. In Amsterdam, a separate statement to this effect was endorsed by Belgium, France, and Italy (with some charges that Germany had helped prevent other EU states to sign such a statement).

12. *In a larger EU, can all member states be equal?* Philip Morris Institute Papers, vol. 9 (April 1996), p. 33.

13. "EU to finance east expansion by growth," Reuters wire, May 14, 1998.

14. Richard Holbrooke, "The United States as a European Power," *Foreign Affairs* 71, no. 2 (March/April 1995).

15. Zbigniew Brzezinski, arguably the most influential geostrategic analyst, helps make the point about the widespread nature of such ambivalence.

The U.S. goal, he wrote in 1997, is to "foster [a] genuine partnership with a more united and politically defined Europe" but, he adds almost at once, "not so politically integrated that it could challenge the United States on matters of geopolitical importance, particularly in the Middle East" (although "unless Europe becomes more united, it is likely to become more disunited again"). "A Geostrategy for Eurasia," *Foreign Affairs* 76, no. 5 (September/October 1997): 53.

16. See, for example, my own "Beyond Bosnia," *Washington Quarterly* 19, no. 3 (Summer 1996). "The 50th anniversary of the Washington Treaty," I wrote there (p. 43), "can be the target date for a first round of [NATO] enlargement likely to include at least most of the states of Central Europe."

17. Sean Kay and Judith Yaffe, "Turkey's International Affairs: Shaping the U.S.-Turkey Strategic Partnership," *Strategic Forum*, no. 122 (July 1997).

18. As stated by Klaus Kinkel, then Germany's foreign minister. Quoted in Lionel Barber and Robert Graham, "The risk of the proposed single currency splitting the European Union," *Financial Times*, March 26, 1997.

PART THREE

Half Before Europe

5

Bridging the Gap
in the Mediterranean

Since the end of the cold war, Western Europe has been caught between two arcs of crises. First, in what used to be described loosely as the East, territorial and ethnic conflicts that had haunted the European continent for centuries have been resurrected, especially in the Balkans. In coming years, these conflicts will continue to demand a forceful display of American leadership, based on U.S. interests and U.S. power. As the American leadership is exerted, however, it may precipitate an especially discordant phase in West-West relations, both within NATO and in the EU and its related institutions (including the Western European Union).

The other arc of crises lies in what was called, just as loosely, the South—a political space broadly defined as that part of the continent where the Ottoman Empire used to end, the Russian empire used to begin, and the European empires in Africa used to start. How historically factual this geographic description is matters less than the fact that it is widely accepted. Extending from Algeria to Turkey, these crises affect mainly Muslim countries in which rejection of the West and its secular institutions is, or may become, the focal point of government policies or their critics. There, the case for an assertive American leadership is not as clear, and asymmetrical interests, expectations, and traditions between EU countries, as well as between them and the United States, may also cause significant tensions in coming years.

Although the nature of the crises on the southern shores of the Mediterranean varies from one place to another, several recurring patterns can be identified from one crisis to the other:

- failed states, some of them stillborn, and a crisis of representativeness in immature democracies, many of them newly born or still in the process of incubation;

- crises of identity in fragmented polities, often established in the aftermath of difficult wars of independence, and conflicts of political legitimacy in unruly societies;

- unfulfilled expectations, conveniently explained by global forces like commodity prices and the discipline imposed by multilateral institutions, but also resulting from, or worsened by, ineffective public policy; and

- disruptive memories of past ethnic clashes from within, and of territorial disputes over boundaries drawn coercively by the colonial powers in earlier years.

In the West, meaning mainly among EU states and in the United States, these issues are viewed differently from country to country. Nonetheless, they can give rise to several processes of potential significance for intra-European and trans-Atlantic relations. Such processes could include

- a renationalization of foreign policies based on the negotiation of separate deals whose short-term gains would take precedence over the long-term costs they might entail;

- deeper EU divisions between a France-led Mediterranean caucus that looks to the South, and a Germany-led northern group that looks to the East, both of which are priority areas for each nation's respective security concerns;

- further complications for the Maastricht-mandated attempts to organize a Common Foreign and Security Policy (CFSP) for Europe; and

- a public disavowal of Western institutions deemed to be tested over issues that they are not equipped to address—including Bosnia—but also said to be defined by such troubling polemics as Turkey's membership in the EU (which is long overdue) and a role for NATO in North Africa (which is occasionally overstated).

Algeria Unhinged

In the 1990s, the Algerian crisis has been fairly typical of the instabilities that have characterized the post–Cold War years: a crisis
inherited from the Cold War but rooted in the long history that
preceded it; a conflict shaped by a difficult and complex agenda
that combines traditional economic and security issues with cultural, religious, and ethnic questions; and a civil war initially neglected
by Western powers whose preoccupation with other crises in the
Balkans and in the Persian Gulf were made especially urgent
because those crises were viewed as more immediately relevant to
their vital interests.[1] The crisis began long before the Cold War, but
even within the limited history of the past 50 years Algeria is a particular case because of the war it waged against France to win independence, and its subsequent efforts to assert its sovereignty.

Several short generations of unmet political projects and societal expectations have thus converged to shape the Algerian crisis of
the past few years. At Evian, France, in 1962, Algerians won a state
before they could reclaim a national identity.[2] The only tie with
their precolonial past, more than 130 years earlier, was Islam; and
their only explicit relationship with, or awareness of, the state's
post-independence leadership of the *Front de Libération Nationale*
(FLN) was war and violence. Ancient memories of heroism helped
sustain a national idea for the 1960s and the early 1970s, among
francisants who viewed the French language as a tool for preserving
some part of their identity north of the Mediterranean, but also
among *arabisants* who wanted to return fully to their Arab origins.

As these memories faded, a new generation of younger
Algerians who had never known colonization rebelled against a cor-
rupted and repressive one-party regime whose leaders were blamed
for Algeria's inability to satisfy economic expectations that had
been raised dramatically after the unexpected rise in oil revenues in
1973. These younger Algerians integrated various Marxist
thoughts—class struggle, socialism, and anti-imperialism—into
Arab nationalist thought and even some Islamic movements.[3]
Despite these emerging radical trends, political dissent remained
muted because the government had the means needed to provide

many of the amenities of a better life (free education, free medical care, employment) as compensation for the lack of democratic fundamentals (political multipartism, free press).[4]

After the death of President Houari Boumediene in December 1979, neither a brilliant but impotent leftist elite nor a less gifted but powerful army—let alone a divided and discredited FLN—could fill the vacuum created by the weakening of the early revolutionary leaders. This role was assumed effectively by Islam as the only organized release for Algerians' anguish and anger. While the state hoped to use Islam as a rampart against the left, Islam emerged as the *état providence* offering the social services that the Algerian government could no longer afford and the democratic outlet that the regime would still not allow. Following a 42 percent fall in oil revenues in 1986, the mosques came under increasing demand not only for religious guidance but also, and more directly, for political expression. When violent urban riots erupted in November 1988, President Chadli Benjedid again turned to Islam as a safety valve, and the measures of liberalization he adopted as a method of crisis management helped give birth to a new party, the *Front Islamique du Salut* (FIS).[5]

From the beginning, the objective of the FIS was not only to sharpen the Islamic identity of Algeria but to make of Algeria a true Islamic state. In the wake of 30 years of ruinous and debilitating independence, the FIS had neither the will nor the patience to be or to become a party-like-any-other, which the regime could consult and manage as an opposition party, and ultimately coopt as a government party. Rather, the FIS became almost instantaneously a mass party: the God-sanctioned populist alternative to an irreversibly tarnished FLN.[6] Yet many of its followers and eventual voters did not identify with the hard core Islamic themes, methods, and objectives that, lacking any other specific program (whether economic or otherwise), the FIS quickly imposed in each of the many districts it won in the local elections of December 1989.[7]

Thus unwilling to be the semi-benevolent partner the regime wanted it to be, but insufficiently organized to govern even after its surprising victory, the FIS could not become a "loyal opposition" after it had been outlawed by the Army. To whom and to what would it be loyal?[8] Certainly not to a regime whose main goal was to eradicate the Front and its supporters. Thus, the strategy of political protest that had worked to the advantage of the FIS was transformed into a strategy of political violence that undermined its status, and even legitimacy, as that violence became more deliberate and indiscriminate.

Admittedly, predictions of Algeria as a radical Islamist republic, made since the aborted national elections of January 1992, have not come to pass.[9] The killing continues, to be sure, but such violence could not force the replacement of President Liamine Zeroual's regime with a government headed by the FIS. Indeed, from one election to the next, the FIS lost much of the popular support it briefly enjoyed at the turn of the 1980s. Now, the electoral triumphs it achieved in 1990 and 1991 are no longer repeatable—whether alone or in alliance with other political parties that are not eager to help the FIS's rehabilitation at the expense of their own political prospects.

The isolation of the FIS also grew out of its open and brutal rift with the *Groupe Islamique Armé* (GIA)—a civil war within the civil war. FIS leaders who joined the GIA in 1994 were summarily killed by their new allies in early 1996. Since then, the FIS leadership has grown divided, embittered by escalating atrocities, frustrated by the government's refusal to negotiate, and no longer courted by foreign governments made more sensitive to the gap between the FIS leaders' rhetoric abroad and the actions pursued in their name at home. Meanwhile, the GIA has become a loose confederation of autonomous groups, politically and psychologically remote from any central leadership and even sophisticated weaponry. Many of these groups, said to represent a few thousand guerrillas, respond to interests that have little to do with Islam and more to do with economic gain and criminal activities. Plain nihilistic tendencies are also shown by field unit commanders whose average age is under 19 and whose life expectancy barely reaches six to nine months from the time they take charge of a unit. Under such conditions, there is little will for restraint. New levels of primitive and dehumanizing brutality are set with each new attack. Targets previously spared might become fair game—especially those of greatest practical significance to the state (like oil and gas pipelines and installations) and of greatest symbolic significance to the fighters (like European and U.S. citizens and assets).[10] Predictably, such escalating terror adds to the confusion, which, in turn, complicates prospects for national reconciliation.

As the populist appeal of FIS has faded, and as the GIA has become identified with intolerable violence, the regime attempted to redirect the FIS constituencies toward other religious parties. Thus, after the other Islamic party, Hamas, participated in the presidential election of November 1995, it was offered and accepted minor posts in the government, and attended the government-sponsored Conference of National Concord of September 1996. With Hamas viewed as a plausible democratic and nonviolent version of the FIS, its leaders helped President Zeroual's limited dialogue on constitutional reforms aimed at the organization of an explicitly secular political system that would limit the executive's authority and the influence of the political parties: a two-term limit for the president, responsible to a constitutional court; an electoral system based on proportional representation and designed to limit the representation in parliament of the larger parties; and the explicit dissociation of religion and ethnicity from political platforms.

Yet, even though Zeroual's election in November 1995 was relatively fair and statistically convincing (if only because of a surprisingly high turnout), the vote did not mean that people had new confidence in his ability to restore peace and order in the country any more than the 1991 result was a vote of confidence in the FIS's democratic credentials. The 1991 national election was a forceful statement of discontent by voters who showed their determination to oust the ruling party. The 1995 election, when the FIS lost about one million votes, confirmed the voters' decision to block the FIS as an alternative—not because they denied Islamic participation in the state but because they rebelled against an Islamic attempt to seize the state by force.[11]

In all instances, voters wanted a new beginning: in 1991, to force the ruling clique out of power, and in 1995, to leave religion out of politics—not because a majority of Algerians had discovered that they could be better off without Islam, but because they had come to realize how much worse off they could be with an Islamist state. In short, the 1991 vote was not for the confrontation that followed, and the 1995 vote was not about a reconciliation that is still awaited. Indeed, the various elections held by Zeroual after November 1995—legislative (June 1997) and local (October 1997), with constitutional referendum (November 1996) in between—did not solve the question of state legitimacy. That was the reason why these elections were held. They would help achieve legitimacy abroad as a belated redemption for the cancellation of the 1991 elections, which was accepted by Western governments because of an underlying assumption that secular forces are by definition more democratic (or, at least, less anti-democratic) and moderate (or, at least, less radical) than an Islamic alternative. But these elections would also help achieve legitimacy at home as a response to the call for unity issued by all political parties, including the FIS, that offered, at San'Egidio in January 1995, a peaceful compromise that the regime has refused to hear because neither Zeroual nor the army wants to risk sharing power with an Islamic party, be it a marginalized FIS or a moderate Hamas. Thus, by defining itself as profoundly secular and irreversibly anti-Islamist, the regime in Algeria became fundamentally anti-democratic because its opponents could not be "eradicated" or even ignored by democratic means.

What is left for the government in the absence of a political opening that might lead to some measure of reconciliation is to make the Algerian economic space more prosperous and more livable. That is not easy either, even for those who escape the daily massacres. The Algerian economy has performed relatively well since 1996, but its limits are known. With most of the country's national income and nearly all of its foreign exchange revenues generated by oil and gas fields located on a narrow territorial base, there are in fact two Algerias: one that is productive and hence usable (the Sahara, the source of most of the country's export earnings) and one that is mainly useless as a consumer of resources.[12] To enter the former, which has been cordoned off by the Army, special passes are needed; to enter the latter, arms and explosives suffice. The oil market upon which the former depends defines the government's tenuous ability to satisfy the needs of the latter: at prevailing export levels, a $1 drop in oil prices results in a $560 million loss in Algeria's annual receipts.[13]

After the 1995 presidential election, solid growth, falling infla-
tion, small budget surpluses and a positive trade balance, and growing reserves reassured potential investors and multilateral lenders
abroad and helped make Zeroual's institutionalized dictatorship
more tolerable at home. Over time, however, such "good" news
could only amount to a short reprieve because it failed to reduce
inequalities and control unemployment (estimated at 47 percent by
1997, including more than 30 percent in direct unemployment).[14]
Under such conditions, Zeroual's decision, in October 1998, to
resign after an early presidential election in the spring of 1999, recognized his inability to improve economic and political conditions
beyond the limited satisfaction provided selectively during the previous two years.

Algeria stands far behind what any "reasonable observer" might
have anticipated 35 years ago.[15] In fact, the opposite claim ignores
the political grounds in which the seeds of the new state were
planted in 1962: a state reborn after 130 years of being a nominal
part of France, where secularity is a religion. Because of this experience, history may show that the Algerian crisis of the 1990s was an
aberration. Its choice for secularity has been confirmed repeatedly
since the FIS called secular democracy blasphemy and waged *jihad*
against it. This is not an emotional judgment, although, admittedly, it contains some emotion. Still, Algeria has become unhinged,
and what will follow for the balance of the decade and into the
next century remains uncertain. However the states of Europe and
the United States care about Algeria—for reasons of self-interest,
alliance cohesion, and sheer compassion—they must remain vigi-
lant. Yet, at a time when key European countries, including France,
are in a fragile state, when the process of European integration faces
an extraordinarily demanding agenda, and when the U.S. role in
the post–Cold War world is ill defined, how can Western vigilance
be exercised?

Which War, Whose Crisis?

The Algerian crisis has unfolded in the shadow of the "savage war
of peace" waged against France to gain independence.[16] For
Algerians who still define themselves in terms of their relations

north of the Mediterranean, Paris is the place where it is especially gratifying to be seen, to have friends, and to be heard. Conversely, for other Algerians who object to these ties, it is the place against which the final war of liberation—intellectual and ideological, as well as cultural and religious—must be waged if Algeria is ever going to be fully independent. In short, the savage war Algerians have been waging on each other since 1992 is "prompted by the same causes, tracing the same contours and unfolding with the same unspeakable brutality" as the war of independence, although it is waged this time not merely against France and its culture but against Western culture, and even, in the end, culture itself.[17]

French memories of *l'Algérie française* are painful memories of political turmoil and physical violence that ultimately brought the Fourth Republic down. As the Algerian crisis moved to the forefront of France's domestic concerns, it has raised questions of race, religion, and ethnicity. Most disturbingly, the crisis has encouraged the mainstream political parties in France to adopt some of the most extreme positions developed by Jean-Marie Le Pen's far-right *Front National*. These positions are designed not only to close the door on further entries of Algerian immigrants but also to force their return to their points of origin.[18]

Many crucial moments of the Algerian crisis have unfolded in the difficult French context of a cohabitation between two adversarial political majorities—in 1986–88, 1993–95, and since 1997. The 1988 riots in Algiers were ignored by then-Prime Minister Jacques Chirac, the neo-Gaullist who was hoping to defeat incumbent President François Mitterrand that fall. In early 1992, suspension of the democratic process and more repression in Algeria produced words of condemnation from Mitterrand, but little else. The following year, another period of *cohabitation* between Mitterrand and conservative Prime Minister Edouard Balladur produced more French aid designed to bolster the regime against its Islamic challengers (as Balladur wanted it), although it would not bolster democracy against the regime (as Mitterrand hoped). Fears that violence might spread to France were confirmed by a wave of terror in the streets of Paris in mid-1995, shortly after Chirac's election to the presidency. Whether such violence grew out of internal conflicts between and within the FIS, the GIA, and the Algerian

Army, or whether it was an explicit Islamic terrorist campaign, it had a dramatic impact on the French public. When winter came, however, the violence ended as suddenly as it had begun, but the French continued to fear more terror that would be inspired abroad and carried out by new French citizens and illegal aliens. In late 1997, nearly 75 percent of the French still viewed the Algerian crisis as a threat to France.[19]

To keep Algeria and its people at a safe distance, the French government has drawn a metaphorical Maginot line that relies on restrictive measures that can reduce, deny, or even reverse the entry of North Africans in France: tougher visa requirements for Algerian nationals who wish to come to France, longer denial of residence papers for undocumented parents of children born in France (and thus, French citizens), fewer approvals of Algerian demands for asylum, and more obstacles to naturalization. In France, as elsewhere in Europe, the debate on immigration has only started. Not surprisingly, such restrictive legislation widens the societal gaps across the Mediterranean and increases societal tensions within France.

Demographic pressures, both factual and perceived, make matters worse. Who is to be counted as a "legal foreigner" varies from one state to the next. In Germany, for example, many or most of the several million "foreigners" have lived in the country for generations without being granted German citizenship. As a result, estimates of "foreigners" vary widely, for the EU at large and for any of its members.[20] In 1993, Spain's police reportedly arrested for criminal activities nearly three times as many Algerians as there were registered Algerian residents in the country.

Such statistics, which are repeated elsewhere, need not be reliable to produce nightmarish images for a credulous public. Even under good economic and political conditions, the Maghreb is not just an underdeveloped region: it is underdeveloping—meaning that disparities from within, as well as between these countries and their wealthier European neighbors are growing. Thus, with annual average growth rates for the Algerian population placed at 3.7 and 4.1 percent during the 1980–1990 and 1990–95 periods respectively, more than 250,000 youths enter the job market in Algeria every year, but barely 50,000 jobs are created in a good year. The risks of explosion are obvious. Four-fifths of the unemployed are under the age of 30, and many of them are moving to the cities, where there is little housing and no work.[21] The two-fifths of all Algerians who are under 14 remain insufficiently educated for the labor force that is needed if Algeria is going to perform in the global economy or for the jobs that may be available in performing foreign economies. Life expectancy is rising steadily (over 68 years in 1996) without a related increase in the state's ability to attend to the needs of the elderly. The foreign investments attracted to Algeria by the discovery of new oil fields and improved political and administrative conditions do not create jobs, and the new revenues generated by more oil exports are earned with a weak dollar that buys fewer imports denominated in strong European currencies.

Muslims in Europe who have escaped the dire conditions that prevail in their countries of origin oppose the more radical Islamic groups and deplore any violence exerted by or against their Islamic brothers, whatever the sources of that violence. The integration to which most of them aspire is delayed or denied by a rising political ambivalence and societal hostility that progressively force Muslim nationals—new immigrants, but also native-born children of older immigrants—into separate communities that may be easily radicalized should these conditions persist and worsen. In late January 1991, two-thirds of all Muslims in France opposed military intervention in Iraq (after the war had started), and one-fourth of these Muslims between the age of 14 and 25 indicated a willingness to fight on the side of Iraq.[22] Significantly enough, many of these are the children of the *harkis* who fought on the side of the French government during the Algerian war of independence.

Evidence of a re-Islamization of Muslim citizens who rebel against these conditions of permanent humiliation abounds throughout Europe. This is no longer about Algeria, but about every part of the Islamic world that has returned to Europe from every part of the world where European states used to rule. These Muslim enclaves, which often rely on largesse from other Muslim states, are passionately condemned as "a characteristically American kind . . . of ethnic identity" that forms an increasingly assertive subculture within the previously dominant national culture.[23] Their distinctive and even conflictual communitarian identities reinforce the perception among non-Muslim citizens in Europe that their Muslim compatriots constitute an Islamic society separate from their own and are the agents of a conspiracy aimed at the West, its institutions and its values.

Beyond such geocultural concerns, other European concerns about Algeria and its neighbors are geoeconomic (with the EU doing more profit-generating business with Mediterranean Arab countries than with Japan) and geopolitical (including a dangerous proliferation of weapons of mass destruction). These concerns need not be faced evenly between all EU states to be shared commonly.

Economic interests in Algeria and the rest of the Maghreb are generally more significant for France than for any other EU country—although with a reduced dependence on imported energy supplies, France ranks only as Algeria's fourth customer (after Germany, the United States, and Italy). About one-fourth of all Algerian imports (including a large proportion of capital goods) come from France, with about 3,000 firms, most of them rather small, involved in these transactions. Many of these firms are located in the region of Provence-Côte d'Azur, which contains the port of Marseilles, one of Le Pen's political strongholds. An important share of Algeria's large debt is owed to French private and public banking institutions, and several leading French companies have invested heavily in Algeria.

Political-security concerns and interests are rooted in geography, fashioned by history, and nurtured by tradition: a pervasive fear of violence exported to Europe from across the Mediterranean, some lingering resentment over the loss of what used to be European, and a cultural self-definition of Europe. Since the end of the Cold War, the most brutal conflicts in Europe have erupted in Muslim-populated areas, and the countries most immediately feared and most persistently courted by the states of Europe outside the European continent have been Muslim countries, including Iraq, Iran, and Libya.

More instability in Algeria and its neighbors would worsen concerns felt in Italy, for example, with reports of possible attacks from Iraq during the Gulf War in early 1991, or in France, when an Air France plane was hijacked in Algiers and reportedly filled with explosives for an attack on Paris in late 1994. The ongoing spread of theater ballistic missiles (TBMs) is especially worrisome. Within the next decade, all the capitals of Southern Europe could be within range of TBMs launched from countries in North Africa and the Middle East, with some able to deliver biological, chemical, or even nuclear weapons (periodically reported to be sought by various Arab states, including Algeria).

Such concerns have increased Europe's interests in surface-to-air missile systems that can intercept TBMs and cruise missiles and that would be preferably developed multilaterally, whether in a European context or through cooperative arrangements with the United States.[24] That capabilities of mass destruction are more likely to be used by a state with an Islamic rather than a secular government is often deemed to be self-evident in European countries that show a troubling cultural bias regarding Muslim countries south of the Mediterranean.

The revolutionary tradition of Algerian leaders, irrespective of their political persuasion, might provide the motivation and reach that other Muslim states that attempted to export their revolution, by secular or Islamic means, have lacked. A radically oriented Islamic regime in Algeria could affect the government of Tunisia's president Zine el-Abidine Ben Ali, whose highly effective economic reforms have come together with strict control of Islamic tendencies and, for that matter, any type of political dissent. The potential for severe internal trouble remains, therefore, real, especially if economic conditions were to deteriorate. East of Tunisia, through Libya and Sudan, a radical Islamist regime or more disorders in Algeria might give existing anti-secular instabilities in Egypt and Saudi Arabia a violent turn in countries where the reality of Western interests is not in question.

Morocco's Alaouite monarchy stands as a rampart against serious spillovers from its neighbors. Yet, radical temptations might cross the border and erode Morocco's well-established moderation in the Middle East, where King Hassan often played the role of broker with much diplomatic skill and considerable personal courage. Such radical temptations might even be felt in the Spanish enclaves of Ceuta and Melilla, neither of which is included in the NATO area and both of which could not expect much support from Spain's EU partners.[25] Finally, with an Islamist government in

Algiers likely to increase its support for the anti-Moroccan Polisario Front in the Western Sahara, an escalation of the war might have significant consequences at a time when King Hassan is pursuing serious and far-reaching political reforms. In all of these cases, the key to Morocco's policies and its stability remains the king, who could easily manage these difficulties, as he has done many times in the past. Nevertheless, persistent reports concerning Hassan's poor health and some uncertainties about his succession serve as pointed reminders that regime stability cannot depend on a single man or institution.

Concerns about the spillovers of the Algerian crisis are not meant to suggest an automatic fall of domino states in, around, and beyond North Africa. Nor do they imply that any conflagration in North Africa, the Middle East, or the Persian Gulf will find its shortest fuse in Algeria.[26] Much can happen that would have worse consequences than events in Algeria—as witnessed, for example, in May 1996 with the elections in Israel, in late 1997 with renewed prospects for war with Iraq, and in June 1998 with a round of nuclear tests in India and Pakistan. In all of these instances, the risk was not the spread of instabilities from Algeria to other Muslim states but the reverse, as could be confirmed after 1999 in the context of new crises in the Persian Gulf with Iraq and a collapse of the Arab-Israeli peace process in the Middle East. Yet, however such risks flow, Algeria must be viewed as a "pivot state"[27]—a critical actor in the evolution of the European Union, the transatlantic security structure, and the search for peace in the Middle East and other regions that include states with a significant Muslim population.

No Will to Lead

France, which boasts of multiple centrality as a Mediterranean, Atlantic, and Northern European country, holds a special interest in North Africa, and its known aspirations for influence in Europe make it a natural candidate for leadership in Algeria, which was made an explicit part of the North Atlantic area when the Washington Treaty was signed in April 1949. In wartime as well as

in time of peace, all French governments have resisted any intervention of other countries in their imperial backyard across the
Mediterranean (and in Africa too). Since the Algerian crisis began,
however, such resistance has receded. More specifically, the French
now handle Algeria like the Alsace-Lorraine of their schooldays:
n'en parler jamais mais y penser toujours.

Most generally, French policies are influenced by some historical guilt (or regrets), racial prejudices (or political correctness), and
economic greed (or relative indifference). This curious blend produces an equally curious mixture of intrusiveness and passivity.
Declining bilateral aid is provided almost anonymously to avoid
perceptions of any condition the Algerian government and its
opposition might use to demonstrate their national credentials.
Such a low profile is designed to avoid a political debate over the
cost of losing, or regaining, France's former influence.

With France neither able nor willing to lead as readily as in the
past, a more active role has been sought by a Mediterranean caucus
of EU states (France, Italy, and Spain, plus Portugal and Greece)
and a few southern states (including Algeria, Morocco, and Tunisia,
as well as Malta, Egypt, and others). This caucus, dubbed "Club
Med," had its best opportunity for influence in the second half of
1995 when France, Spain, and Italy formed the EU's ruling troika
of the previous, current, and next presidents of the European
Council.

As could have been expected, however, even within such a limited Club Med, different national interests and political aspirations
among the EU states and their neighbors stood in the way of any
lasting common policies. Unlike France, for example, Spain's memories are more closely tied to Morocco (a central feature of the
post-Franco succession, and the last site of Spain's colonial past)
than to Algeria, but its economic interests are more centered in
Algeria (which is the source of nearly 70 percent of Spain's natural
gas) than in Tunisia or the rest of the Arab world. For Italy, the
Maghreb countries that matter most—on grounds of gas, investments, and growing flows of unwanted immigrants—are Tunisia
and Libya, but Italian attention has been diverted by increasing
instabilities and audible rumors of war in the Balkans around
Kosovo, and in the Aegean around Cyprus.

Not surprisingly, these differences between the Mediterranean countries obstruct multilateral policies for the region, and 18 months of Mediterranean leadership, including a summit of the European Council held in Barcelona in September 1995, showed only modest results in three areas.[28] First, enforcement of the Schengen agreement produced some coordination on asylum and immigration, as well as on organized crime and drug smuggling: in Spain, where the numbers of northward-bound Moroccans were reduced, and in Italy, where an informal coalition between the ex-Communists, the federalist Northern League, and the neo-Fascists has been generally supportive of various legislative measures designed to expel thousands of illegal immigrants.[29]

In addition, the EU commitment made in Barcelona for a free trade area (FTA) with North Africa produced a series of bilateral accords with each of the countries involved, pending a comprehensive multilateral framework by the year 2010. Agriculture, however, has remained excluded from these agreements, and an FTA with former dependencies in the South may clash with EU enlargement to the East—not only over budgetary issues but also because of the concessions that will be made to applicant countries from the East prior to their accession. Accordingly, the FTA's first goal is to increase trade among southern Mediterranean countries, which remains virtually insignificant, and assist them with soft loans, which are still far too modest.

Finally, Club Med planning envisions a common security space protected by at least two European land- and sea-based forces led by France, with participation from Spain and Italy (Eurofor and Euromarfor). These forces, however, will require many years before they become operational, if ever. Admittedly, Euro-Atlantic security organizations have been gaining western, northern, and southern coherence—with Spain joining the Eurocorps and France bargaining for its return to NATO's integrated military structures. Yet, like every other attempt by EU countries to develop common policies and build common forces, within or outside the EU, the availability of NATO assets (including surveillance and transport), U.S. power (including its Sixth Fleet), and even U.S. leadership (that can produce followership from at least some EU states) will remain indispensable for any significant European action in the

Mediterranean.[30] In 1999 and beyond, Europe's need for U.S. and NATO support will be confirmed by declining defense budgets in the leading EU states, no shared will for military action, no lasting consensus for economic sanctions or any other nonmilitary forms of collective action, and, last but hardly least, the multiplicity of crises ahead—including Kosovo, Cyprus, the Persian Gulf, and the Arab-Israeli conflict.

Even if it is agreed that Algeria is unique, that the Algerian crisis is mainly homegrown, that automatic spillovers of instability from Algeria to its neighbors are unlikely, and that the current regime is now beyond the reach of the extremists, too much is at stake for the United States to be dismissive of, or reactive to, North Africa, as was the case during the Cold War.[31] Not the least of what is at stake is Europe's view of America's reliability, and even the Arab view of America's global sensibilities. In 1995, bilateral talks that were held between Paris and Washington to review U.S. support for a hypothetical French-led evacuation of its citizens, as well as those of other foreign countries, from Algeria, were especially constructive because of the will for dialogue both sides showed.[32] They reduced earlier French fears that the U.S. characterization of the Algerian regime as a "ruling elite" that hangs on to power "tenaciously" and with "little in the way of political liberties" reflected a naked attempt to come to a separate deal in Algiers at France's expense.[33] These negotiations may even have helped facilitate a bilateral rapprochement in Bosnia that summer, and over NATO that winter. In 1996, President Clinton reportedly wrote at least two letters to President Zeroual urging him to seek an "inclusive" reconciliation.[34] In 1997, former secretary of state James Baker was actively involved in a UN-sponsored search for a peace agreement in and over the Sahara. In late 1998, the United States held its first-ever bilateral military exercise with Algeria. What may be most significant in all such examples, among others, is the implicit French acquiescence to, and support for, an enhanced U.S. role in the region.

The cycle of elections held in Algeria since 1995 gave the regime some constitutional legitimacy while eroding much of the Islamists' earlier populist appeal. Periodic elections feed the illusion at least of democratic procedures that are reinforced by occasional expressions of a democracy at work—like the public demonstrations held against electoral frauds after every such election. Yet, Zeroual hardly delivered on his pledge of "consultative dialogue" made when he needed more support from the multilateral financial institutions before the 1995 presidential election: consultation remained explicitly selective, and there was very little in the way of a dialogue. Rising violence, too, served to preempt whatever legitimate claims might have been made by the Islamists: on the whole, the origins of the butchery in Algeria are known, even when its reasons remain incomprehensible. Yet, the indifference of the army to much of the massacre is also known: its passivity suggests some complicity, or at least an indifference, that is also unacceptable.

Whether with or after Zeroual, the Algerian regime will not bridge the gap between the authority it holds and the legitimacy it wants until nonparticipation in the democratic process is a choice that political parties and groups make on their own; and until all those who contribute to the violence act to control and end it. In 1999, external pressures to this effect will be most effective if they are applied by more than one country or one of the institutions to which it belongs—whether France, the traditional leader in the region, or the United States, the natural world leader since 1991; whether the EU, a natural provider of affluence, or NATO, the designated provider of security. Admittedly, conditionality is easier to recommend than to implement. To be effective, it must satisfy criteria of will and vulnerability: the will, that is, for several influential states to impose a price on the target that refuses to accept their conditions, as well as the target's vulnerability to that price. Conditionality also raises issues of timing and substance: when to link the extension of aid, which reforms to emphasize first, how their enforcement can be guaranteed, and how to balance the threat of withdrawal and the promise of rewards.

In short, conditionality is an interventionist gamble that presupposes a consensus based on two assumptions. First, it assumes that the changes sought as "conditions" for support are preferable to what may or will happen unless the recommended changes are adopted—and, not insignificantly, that an interest in such changes is common, although not commonly shared, by and for all the parties. Second, conditionality assumes that the consequences for the target states of ignoring these conditions are lesser than the consequences of changing their behavior—with enough specificity and enough certainty to facilitate acceptance.

On all grounds, this is not an easy gamble for those who initiate the process or for those who give in to it. After the 1995 presidential election, an improving economy left the Algerian regime less sensitive to warnings of denials (of credits, access to markets, or political support). Its resistance to conditionality was all the more convincing as the threat of comprehensive sanctions lacked credibility: in 1996, Algeria recorded a foreign trade surplus of $4.3 billion, which grew to $5.7 billion in 1997. Still, there comes a time when the inability to do much should not constrain one's ability to speak more: on behalf of the citizens, who need protection against violence, whatever its source, and toward national reconciliation with all—including the FIS, because of what it represents rather than because of what it has done or what was done in its name.

In addition, an effective Euro-Atlantic policy toward Algeria must contain the risks of spillover in neighboring countries. The states of Europe and the United States should therefore provide more tangible support for countries like Morocco and Tunisia. A good policy for Algeria begins with sound policies for its two neighbors in North Africa. The U.S. interest in North Africa continues to oscillate between long periods of total indifference and sudden bursts of panic because discussion of this region is often hijacked by other issues not directly related to that region or any single country in the region.

Europe and the United States should also develop closer ties between countries on both sides of the Mediterranean with, for example, separate WEU and NATO Dialogues for Stability, and EU Partnerships for Prosperity that link some countries on the southern shores of the Mediterranean with Euro-Atlantic institutions. The need for an active discussion of such ties is especially significant when decisions about to be made on the EU and NATO will lock these institutions in place for many years to come.

The United States and Europe should state their open support for political reforms that accommodate opposition parties (in Egypt, for instance, but also, arguably, in Tunisia), or for security policies that provide enough satisfaction for regional adversaries (from Israel, for example, but also, arguably, for Turkey) rather than succumbing to implicit blackmail that justifies ineffective government methods and policies with the alleged threat of anti-Western fundamentalism. They should also coordinate policies toward "rogue" regimes (especially those in Iran, Iraq, and Libya). Such policies should include, first, a reappraisal of dual containment in the Persian Gulf, which pleases no ally and shows little result; second, an end to the imposition of unilateral sanctions that open tensions among allies rather than close conflicts with adversaries; and third, agreements on procedures preventing the sales of weapons of mass destruction and the export of related technologies, which bring security to no one and increase instability for all.

Finally, Europe and the United States should link Europe to U.S. initiatives in the Middle East so that the Europeans do not have to challenge U.S. initiatives to demonstrate that they have policies of their own, but also so that Americans do not have to wait for their policies to succeed before being able to rely on support from, and contributions by, the countries of Europe and their Union.

An institutional mechanism that would enable Western countries to coordinate their policies on such questions as the Algerian crisis is still missing. On out-of-area, out-of-Europe issues, the United States and Europe often seem more willing to upstage each other than to consult and cooperate. Unilateral U.S. actions designed to solve regional conflicts that affect EU states (as is the case in North Africa) or NATO states (in the Aegean Sea) suffer from the limits of U.S. will and credibility. Expressions of EU unilateralism to settle local disputes on its own (as was to be the case in Bosnia) are similarly limited by EU capabilities and influence.

Nor are European, Mediterranean, and transatlantic troikas the answer to the need for consultation. The EU troika, which groups the three presidents of the European Council (past, present, and future), responds to the alphabetical listing of EU countries that determines these assignments: some troikas are more effective than others, depending on participating countries. The Mediterranean troika (France, Italy, and Spain) is externally divided and internally weak: in these countries especially, issues pertaining to North Africa have a domestic dimension that makes policy coordination among them difficult irrespective of an insufficiency of available means of action, whether military or otherwise. Finally, the transatlantic troika—which includes the presidents of the United States, the European Commission, and the European Council—is undermined by the short mandate of the European Council presidency (six months, unless a national election makes the term even shorter), and the vagaries of EU agreement on naming the Commission president.

Whether in the Mediterranean or elsewhere, the first five years of the post–Cold War era have confirmed that the operational weaknesses and fragmentation of EU institutions make close cooperation with the United States imperative: the EU has neither the will nor the means to lead. A Transatlantic Action Group consisting of the four or five most influential NATO and EU countries could effectively address out-of-area issues involving NATO and EU states. Patterned after the Contact Group developed for Bosnia (but without Russia), this group would remain sufficiently flexible to include other EU and NATO countries, based on the issue at stake, and activate a process of Transatlantic Policy Coordination comparable to the process of European Political Cooperation that was launched by the then-six members of the European Community in the late 1960s. The goal would be to make consultations possible before decisions are made; these consultations would aim at preparing at least the first draft of a Western policy that would distribute responsibilities and roles in the context of impending crises.

No policy coordination between Europe and the United States can work without better policy coordination within Europe. Fulfillment of the Maastricht-mandated goal of a Common Foreign and Security Policy (CFSP) remains, therefore, imperative: either as the most visible venue for *relance* should the future of Economic and Monetary Union (EMU) be at risk, or as the most compelling venue for an institutional endgame in the afterglow of EMU success. In truth, the formulas that might be envisaged for the CFSP seem less draconian than the steps undertaken on behalf of EMU. Compared to the euro, and compared to the organization of a European Central Bank, agreement on having a single voice speak for Europe looks benign. The Algerian crisis would not be the only issue on Europe's agenda. But relative to Bosnia, Northern Ireland, islets in the Aegean Sea, Cyprus, post-Yeltsin Russia, Ukraine or the Baltic states, and the Persian Gulf or the Middle East peace process, Algeria may be a crisis that Europe can address in common most readily, and through which the gap between the United States and the states of Europe in the Mediterranean can be bridged most effectively.

Notes

1. Claire Spencer, "Algeria in Crisis," *Survival* 36, no. 2, (Summer 1994): 152.

2. Hugh Roberts, "The Algerian State and the Challenge of Democracy," *Government and Opposition* (Autumn 1992): 442.

3. Paul Salem, "The Rise and Fall of Secularism in the Arab World," *Middle East Policy* 4, no. 3 (March 1996): 153. Also, Walter Laqueur, *Communism and Nationalism in the Middle East* (London: Routledge, 1961), 31–36.

4. From the early 1960s to the mid-1980s, Algeria outperformed all other regions in the world except East Asia in income growth per capita, life expectancy growth, and literacy rates, among other leading economic indicators. Phebe Marr, "Swords into Plowshares: The Middle East Economic Challenge, *Mediterranean Quarterly* 8, no. 2 (Spring 1997): 177.

5. Gilles Kepel, "Mouvements islamistes et frustration démocratique" (Islamist movements and democratic frustrations), *Géopolitique*, no. 42 (Summer 1993): 23–24; Khalid Duran, "The Second Battle of Algiers," *Orbis* 33, no. 3 (Summer 1989); Alfred Sherman, "Algeria—An Intellectual Fashion Revisited," *World Today* 45, no. 1 (January 1989). Mustapha K. Al Sayyid, "Slow Thaw in the Arab World," *World Policy Journal* 8 (Fall 1991): 717. Barbara Conry, "North Africa on the Brink," *Mediterranean Quarterly* (Winter 1997): 119. Hamou Amirouche, "Algeria's Islamist Revolution: The People Versus Democracy?" *Middle East Policy* 5, no. 4 (January 1998): 89.

6. Graham Fuller, *Algeria, The Next Fundamentalist State?* (Santa Monica, Calif.: RAND, 1996), 97.

7. The extraordinary speed with which the FIS organized itself into a mass movement left no time to articulate any specific program. Hence the ability to deny or argue that the FIS was no more than "a radical nationalist

party that articulated its policies in the context of Islamism" and, therefore, did not introduce any "dramatically draconian social measures." Michael Willis, *The Islamist Challenge in Algeria: A Political History* (New York: New York University Press, 1997), and Martin Stone, *The Agony of Algeria* (New York: Columbia University Press, 1997). See the review of these books by Barbara Smith, "Algeria: The Horror," *New York Review of Books* 45, no. 7 (April 23, 1998): 27.

8. Mumtaz Ahamd and I. W. Zartman, "Political Islam: Can It Become a Loyal Opposition?" *Middle East Policy* 5, no. 1 (January 1997): 74.

9. Edward G. Shirley, "Is Iran's Present Algeria's Future?" *Foreign Affairs* 74, no. 3 (May/June 1995): 28–44.

10. "No winners in Algeria's endgame," *Middle East Economic Digest* 39, no. 15 (April 14, 1995): 3. Phebe Marr, "The United States, Europe, and the Middle East: An Uneasy Triangle," *Middle East Journal* 48, no. 2 (Spring 1994): 213. Such retargeting of the GIA would be especially significant because U.S. citizens and firms have usually been protected from violence since Algeria's independence—whether physical, as now, or ideological, as was the case when a socialist Algeria, eager to lead the nonaligned states, allowed U.S. investments to achieve preeminence in leading economic sectors, to the irritation of other French companies.

11. Yahia Zoubir, "Algeria: the ballot box versus the bullet," *Jane's Defence Weekly* 25, no. 6 (February 7, 1996); I. William Zartman, "Algeria After the Election: A Giant Small Step," *CSIS Africa Notes*, no. 186, July 1996; Robert Mortimer, "Islamists, Soldiers and Democrats: The Second Algerian War," *Middle East Journal* 50, no. 1 (Winter 1996): 25.

12. Interview of Gilles Kepel, by Dominique Dhombres, *Le Monde*, February 11, 1997.

13. The price for Algerian Saharan blend fell from $20 a barrel in October 1997 to around $11 a barrel by November 1998, as compared with the $18 assumed by the government in preparing its 1998 budget and the $15 envisioned for the 1999 budget. Roula Khalaf, "Algerian regime smiles grimly through oil price headache," *Financial Times* (March 11, 1998): 10, and Jean-Pierre Tuquoi, "L'équilibre du budget algérien compromis" (Algeria's budgetary balance compromised), *Le Monde*, November 11, 1998.

14. J. P. Tuquoi, "L'économie algérienne" (The Algerian economy), *Le Monde*, October 23, 1997; Ghiles Francis, "Réformes économiques" (Economic reforms), *Le Monde*, May 29, 1997; Anthony Cordesman, *Algeria and the Mahgreb* (Washington, D.C.: Center for Strategic and International Studies, January 1998); "Algeria Gains a Vote of Confidence with Foreign Oil Contracts" *New York Times*, December 21, 1995; and "Total and Repsol Sign $850m Gas Deal with Algeria," *New York Times*, January 30, 1996. These

improvements should be placed in some context: during the period 1985–1995, Algeria's annual rate of economic growth was negative (-2.4 percent a year) compared to a +0.9 growth rate in Morocco. During that same period, the terms of trade fell from 173 to 83 (as compared to Morocco, where they fell slightly from 99 to 90). Alain Féler and Oussama Kanaan, "An Assessment of Macroeconomic and Structural Adjustment in the Middle East and North Africa Since 1980," *Middle East Policy* 5, no. 1 (January 1997): 102. Net private capital flows went from $897 million to $129 million in 1995 (with $731 and $572 millions as the corresponding figures in Morocco). *World Development Report*, 1997, 214, 216, 218.

15. As suggested in William H. Lewis, "Algeria at 35: The Politics of Violence," *Washington Quarterly* 19, no. 3 (Summer 1996): 3–18.

16. Alistair Horne, *A Savage War of Peace. Algeria, 1954–1962* (London: Macmillan, 1977).

17. Malise Ruthven, "The Islamist Movement in the Middle East and North Africa," *The Middle East and North Africa* (London: Europa Publications, 1997), 4th ed., 13.

18. In mid-1996, 28 percent of the French people described themselves in agreement with Le Pen's ideas, compared to 19 percent two years earlier. See "Plus d'un français sur quatre d'accord avec les idées du Front national" (More than one Frenchman out of four in agreement with the ideas of the National Front) and "L'influence des idées du FN connaît sa plus forte progression depuis 1990" (The influence of the ideas of the FN registers its strongest progression since 1990), *Le Monde*, April 3, 1996.

19. *Le Monde*, September 12, 1997.

20. The past French practice of giving citizenship to anyone born in French territory—which used to include Algeria (and other overseas outposts in the Caribbean, Pacific, and Indian Ocean)—has left tens of thousands of Algerians in Algeria with dual citizenship, at least nominally. How irresistibly tempting it is to recall de Gaulle's comment, reportedly made to Alain Peyrefitte, shortly before the French withdrawal from Algeria: "Have you been to see the Muslims, with their turbans and jelabas? You can see they are not French. . . . People who talk about integration have pigeons' brains. . . . How can we stop them coming to France and settling in our cities . . . ? My village would no longer be called Colombey-les-Deux-Eglises, but Colombey-les-Deux-Mosquées."

21. *World Development Report, 1997*, 220.

22. W. De Wenden, in W. A. R. Shadid and P. S. Konigsveld, *Muslims in the Margin, Political Responses to the Presence of Muslims in Western Europe* (Kemper, Netherlands: Kok Pharos Publishing House, 1996), 60.

23. Olivier Roy, "Islam in France," in Bernard Lewis and Dominique Schnapper, *Muslims in Europe* (London: Pinter Publishers, 1994), 55.

24. Ian O. Lesser and Ashley J. Tellis, *Strategic Exposure: Proliferation Around the Mediterranean* (Santa Monica, Calif.: RAND, 1996) and *Security in North Africa: Internal and External Challenges* (Santa Monica, Calif.: RAND, 1993), 50–52. At the Ain Oussera complex, about 130 kilometers south of Algiers, a nuclear reactor of Chinese origin is reportedly able to produce enough plutonium for a nuclear weapons program. John Deutch, "The New Nuclear Threat," *Foreign Affairs* 71, no. 4 (Fall 1992): 131–132.

25. Kenneth W. Estes, "Spain's View of Maghreb as NATO's Southern Flank," *Jane's International Defense Review* 29 (January 1, 1996): 20.

26. One observer has spoken of Algeria as "the first of many insurrections which may erupt in Egypt, Tunisia, Morocco, Jordan, Saudi Arabia and Iraq"—and the author adds, should this row of dominoes be insufficient, "for starters." Peter St. John, "Insurgency in Algeria: War Without End," Occasional Paper, Center for Defence and Security Studies, University of Manitoba, April 1996, p. 2.

27. Robert S. Chase, Emily B. Hill, and Paul Kennedy, "Pivotal States and U.S. Strategy," *Foreign Affairs* 75, no. 1 (January-February 1996): 33–51.

28. Roberto Aliboni, "Multilateral Political Cooperation in the Mediterranean" and "Institutionalizing Mediterranean Relations," Istituto Affari Internazionali, *Documenti IAI* no. 9409, September 1994, and 9505, March 1995. Club Med accomplishments are limited, relative to the EU's ambitious objectives of political stability, balanced and sustained economic growth, and conflict resolution and management. Saleh M. Nsouli, Amer Bisat, and Oussana Kanaan, "The EU's New Mediterranean Strategy," *Finance and Development* (September 1996): 14.

29. "No Room at the Inn," *Economist*, December 9, 1995, 53.

30. NATO Secretary General Willy Claes caused considerable controversy in early 1995 when he described Islamic fundamentalism as "at least as dangerous as communism used to be to the West." *Süddeutsche Zeitung*, February 1, 1995.

31. Graham Fuller is right to fall in a repetitive mode when discussing the U.S. and Western stakes in Algeria. Perhaps this is, indeed, the only way to be heard. Thus, the phrase "The stakes are . . . high" opens and concludes Fuller's short book, *Algeria: The Next Fundamentalist State?*, pages 1 and 119.

32. These talks reportedly included contingency plans for flying in troops (mostly French and none American) to secure oil and gas installations and bring out expatriate staff (including 500 or so American nationals)—possibly as had been done earlier in a few countries in Africa (although on a smaller scale than that contemplated for Algeria). Michael Sheridan, "US and France prepare for Algerian evacuation," *Independent*, March 22, 1995.

33. Mark Parris, acting assistant secretary of state for Near Eastern affairs, *Hearings*, House Foreign Affairs, Africa Subcommittee, March 22, 1994.

Later that year, officials refused to link the hijacking of an Air France jetliner to the Islamic groups that had claimed the action. Thomas W. Lippman, "To Islam, an Olive Branch," *Washington Post*, December 28, 1994.

34. *Dallas Morning News*, January 5, 1997.

6

Bridging the Gulf across the Atlantic

THROUGHOUT THE COLD WAR, many of the most serious disagreements between the United States and its allies in Europe grew out of crises outside Europe. At first, conflicts in the Third World that involved the states of Europe were criticized in the United States for giving the West a bad name. Decades later, when colonial empires had disappeared, it was the turn of the United States to be criticized for policies that sought to assert and enhance U.S. influence relative to that of the Soviet Union in regions that were often indifferent or hostile to both superpowers.

To be sure, dissension among the states of Europe was always as important as divisions between them and the United States, except when European unity could be achieved at the expense of U.S. leadership. Yet, to assume that transatlantic and intra-European differences outside Europe have subsided now that the Cold War is over would be to assume that these differences were primarily a reflection of the Cold War. The opposite may well be true. The collapse of the Soviet Union and the threat raised by its power has made the United States and the states of Europe even less tolerant of their differences over issues that raise questions of interests as well as of values: interests whose urgency is not felt evenly, and values whose relevance is perceived differently on the two sides of the Atlantic, and among the European states.

Nowhere are these divisions more enduring than in the Greater Middle East, that is, "the huge area from North Africa through Egypt, Israel and the Tigris-Euphrates valley, through the Persian Gulf region into Turkey and on to the Caspian basin."[1] This is an area in which the countries of Europe have traditionally had major political and economic interests. For each EU state, the country or area of primary interest within the Middle East may differ, but the concerns of all EU states remain broadly the same, including a persistent concern over U.S. leadership and use of power in the region.

Thus, during the Cold War, Europeans repeatedly held the United States, rather than the Soviet Union, responsible for the crises that threatened Europe's access to Arab oil, beginning with the Suez crisis (1956), and including the first and second oil crises (1973 and 1980) and even the Gulf wars between Iran and Iraq (1980–88) and with Iraq (1991). Europeans also blamed the United States for making Israel the U.S. primary interest in the region (raising serious Arab concerns about American even-handedness), for its blind assistance to the shah of Iran as the guardian of the Gulf, and for its initial support of Saddam Hussein's Iraq as the rampart against the Islamic regime in Iran after the fall of the shah.[2]

Since the overwhelming display of U.S. power and leadership during the 1991 war against Iraq, differences between the allies outside Europe have been especially visible in the Persian Gulf. These differences, however, have usually not been over goals, about which there has been widespread agreement: namely, preventing the proliferation of weapons of mass destruction, deterring the spread of terrorism, avoiding the interruption of oil supplies and the manipulation of oil prices, sustaining the peace process between Israel and the Arab states, and often, but not always, protecting and enhancing human rights. Given broad agreement about such goals, disagreements have emerged over the choice of policies most likely to help achieve them, especially when these policies might entail the use of military force, or more precisely, U.S. military force.[3]

Europe's Interests in the Persian Gulf

How to contain radical states in the Greater Middle East is not an easy question. Europe's preference for dialogue, whether with Iran and Iraq, with the Palestinians rather than with the Israelis, or with any of the more radical Arab states (including Libya, the Sudan, and Syria), is based on a number of vital interests. All those interests—politicocultural, as well as economic and strategic—give the Persian Gulf region specifically, and the Greater Middle East more generally, unparalleled significance, especially now that the EU states can take their security in Europe for granted.

The politicocultural interest is rooted in Europe's long association with Islam as a civilization, and with Muslims as a people. Historically, this relationship has often been conflictual. In the twentieth century, Europeans have used force and diplomacy to draw boundaries, create states, install rulers, and educate elites in order to assert their control and maintain their influence in the region. Even today, many in the Arab world still view the countries of Europe in terms of their historical role in the region: France and Great Britain as the traditional great powers with mixed records of imperial involvement; Germany as the business partner *par excellence* because of its failure to acquire a share of the European empires; Italy and Spain, once imperial states in their own right, but now smaller and subdued states with interests that are linked to the region primarily because of proximity; and Russia, whose imperial memories provide the potential for mischief but whose interest has to do with its multicultural identity as a patchwork state (including a sizeable Muslim community).[4]

As we have seen in the specific context of the Algerian crisis, European interests in the Greater Middle East also stem from increased immigration from Islamic countries. Over the years, large numbers of Muslims have settled in different parts of Europe—an estimated 2.6 million Turks in Germany (and many others in Holland), about three million Algerians in France, and uncertain numbers of Moroccans in Spain, Italy, and Belgium. Islam has now become an increasingly contentious issue for Europeans who rebel against the continued erosion of their national identities, which started during the Cold War in the name of "the West" (to save it from communism), and has been intensified since the Cold War in the name of "Europe" (to protect it from nationalism).

The potential for radicalization of Muslim groups in some EU states is real. Whether citizens or immigrants, locally born children of legal immigrants (with or without citizenship), or illegal foreigners (with even less hope of gaining legal status), many Muslims who live in Europe are a new generation of national misfits, living at the margin of their country of adoption—often denied citizenship or threatened with losing their passport or whatever official document they may have.[5] In each Muslim community in Europe, there are signs of re-Islamization as a reaction to these conditions of permanent humiliation: Turkish or Ottoman flags that hang in the ever larger number of local mosques, older Muslims who insist on being buried in their home country, proliferating Koranic schools that draw on explicitly religious teaching materials, Islamic law that is applied to personal and family matters. With the conditions that prompt such trends generally ignored by local authorities and national governments, support and guidance come from other states and/or religious authorities abroad. In thousands of mosques or religious sites in France and Germany, prayers said in Arabic by clerics named in Riyadh or in Ankara are heard but not understood by young Muslims who no longer speak the language and are not recognized as citizens by the Islamic countries in which they were born and to which they do not wish to return.

The growing presence of Islam in Europe is only one of several reasons why Europe has an interest in the Greater Middle East. Significant, too, is Europe's dependence on reliable energy supplies at reasonable prices, as well as access to export markets that ensure its ability to pay for its energy imports. Admittedly, European levels of energy dependence vary because some states have effectively diversified their energy sources, or can rely on non-Middle Eastern foreign suppliers, or even have domestic sources of their own. Irrespective of their differences, however, there is little doubt that all European states will continue to need the large quantities of oil imports at predictable prices provided by the region, including Iran (whose current production is absorbed mainly by Europe and Japan) and Iraq, a likely beneficiary of an increase in demand for oil during the next decade.

The region is also an important source of commerce. During the 10 years that followed the 1973 oil crisis, European exports to the Middle East nearly doubled and continued to increase even when oil prices began to fall in 1985. With full employment no longer a fact of life in Europe's welfare states, and with the prevailing levels of economic growth within Europe insufficient to create enough new jobs, the quest for larger shares of foreign markets intensified, with all kinds of bilateral agreements and regional trade preferences designed to respond to the oil-rich states' interest in developing more diverse economies.

On the basis of conditions in the late 1990s, neither Iran nor Iraq is an important market for Europe.[6] It is their long- term potential, however, rather than the modest trade or earnings they can generate now, that is being targeted. European firms that find few investment opportunities in Eastern Europe, and even fewer in Africa, and face too much competition in the Far East have identified these Gulf countries as two of their most lucrative prospects.

Iraq and Iran are geographically close, historically known, and politically open to special relationships with European countries. Iran has one-and-a-half times the population of all Gulf states combined, including Iraq. The year before its Islamic revolution and its war with Iraq (1980–88), Iran's imports amounted to $14.1 billion, and during the two years preceding the 1990–91 Gulf War, Iraq's imports averaged nearly $10 billion. Although Iraq's per capita income has significantly fallen since 1989, memories of a time when it peaked at approximately $14,000 serve as a benchmark for assessing the country's needs for reconstruction, which some estimate at $140 billion. Reportedly, letters of intent are actively solicited by European firms that hope to have, after the sanctions on Iran and Iraq have been lifted, the sort of political and economic advantage over their U.S. competitors that they lack elsewhere.[7]

Predictably, this economic bait is effectively manipulated by both Iran and Iraq. Thus, they publicly reduce their conflict with the West to American hegemonic ambitions in the Gulf, and allege a lack of U.S. understanding of their region's history. European states that harbor misgivings of their own about U.S. leadership worldwide eagerly respond to calls for a dialogue, which is made "constructive" by the prospects of a privileged relationship. Thus, Iraq's Nahr 'Uman and Majun oil fields are earmarked for France's corporate giants, Total and Elf, in return, reportedly, for informal help to end the UN embargo on trade with Iraq that has been in place since 1990.[8] In Iran (whose proven reserves amount to 9 percent of the world oil reserves and 15 percent of the world's gas reserves), Total invested $2 billion in the development of the Sirri oil and gas fields after Conoco was forced to abandon a nearly concluded deal that would have been the first between Iran and a U.S. oil company since 1980.[9]

Transactions of this type exacerbate the differences between Europe and the United States, but they also undermine relations between states in Europe: with Germany, for example, complaining of France's reluctance to pursue a more forceful policy toward Iran, Great Britain complaining that both Germany and France are reluctant to pursue a more forceful policy toward Iraq, and France complaining of its two allies' unwillingness to follow its lead as that of Europe. In truth, all three states remain permanently ready to hide behind their partners' reluctance to act to explain their own passivity, even as each of them exploits its partners' difficult situation to its own economic advantage.

Another major European concern has to do with traditional security issues raised by the availability of weapons of mass destruction (WMD) for rogue regimes that are located in close proximity to Europe. That Iran has chemical weapons facilities, may be developing biological weapons, has purchased Scud-C missiles and long-range SU-24 strike aircraft, and can be assumed to have the ability and resources to produce a crude atomic bomb as part of an active nuclear program, has not escaped Europe's attention. The belated discovery of Iraq's prewar military arsenal, reportedly months away from having one nuclear weapon in January 1991, worries every European state concerned about Saddam Hussein's ability to hide the prohibited components for such a weapon.[10] Europe is also apprehensive about the chemical and biological weapons that could remain undetected despite the UN inspectors' significant efforts to destroy them.

European states that are physically small and densely populated are vulnerable to wholesale terrorism with WMD or conventional and even primitive weapons. With Islam already a cause for local political tensions, these apprehensions provide short-term gains for extremist European political parties. In the long term, warnings of an imminent clash of civilizations could be self-fulfilling, as the Muslim citizens of EU states are being portrayed by many in their country of adoption as agents of a conspiracy against Western institutions and Western values. Radical parties of the Right, such as the National Front in France, have redefined the security dilemma in Europe as one caused from within by immigrant workers who are perceived as primarily Arab, Muslim, and fundamentalist. Islam is thus identified as a destructive force hostile to each Western state and the entire Western civilization.

The Limits of Dual Containment

Critical dialogue with Iran, said French President Jacques Chirac in March 1996, is "not open and friendly, as it would be with countries with whom we have normal trade, cultural, and political relations. . . . [It is] a limited, organized dialogue, through which the Europeans convey to Iran a certain number of ideas, notably in the area of human rights."[11] Europe's interest in a critical dialogue is to manage the totality of its relations with Iran through a combination of political visits (often at the next to highest levels), parliamentary exchanges, international conferences, trade fairs and corporate partnerships, state insurance for exports, new credits designed to increase trade and investments, concessions on the repayment of Iran's debts and, in the case of Iraq, informal pledges of support for the softening and ultimately the lifting of sanctions.

The logic of preserving one's ability to talk may be compelling because of the interests the dialogue addresses, and the perceived vulnerability of its interlocutors to the absence of a dialogue. Rhetoric apart, however, the dialogue has little to show for its efforts, which are often dismissed by the United States as appeasement.[12] For example, after Germany increased its line of credit to Iran between 1989–92, the volume of trade between the two countries fell steadily. In 1996, trade between the two nations amounted to one-quarter of what it had been in 1992, and to nearly half what it had been in 1994. The same has been true of Iran's trade with other major European states. Outside of trade, results have not been any more compelling. In April 1997, Germany's Foreign Minister Klaus Kinkel had a list of "positive results" that included Iran's adoption of the Chemical Weapons Convention, its approval of the extension of the Nuclear Nonproliferation Treaty, and a more moderate discourse about Salman Rushdie (whose death sentence, initially imposed in 1989 for his Satanic Verses, and reaffirmed in 1992, was canceled in 1998).[13] Even for Kinkel, that was not enough to prevent a decision by Germany and all EU states to recall their ambassadors after the German courts accepted the evidence of Iran's involvement, at the highest levels of government, in the 1993 assassination of four Kurdish leaders in Germany.[14]

Europeans, too, deplore U.S. Gulf policies, including sanctions and periodic military attacks that have little to show for the pain they impose on the citizens of these states and the risks of reprisals from their rogue regimes or related groups. Such policies, they allege, are designed to contain domestic critics in the United States more than foreign adversaries in the Gulf. Still, the threat of unilateral sanctions imposed by the U.S. Congress is not ignored by European firms whose presence in the Gulf region is affected accordingly. Not surprisingly, governments in Tehran and Baghdad take U.S. warnings seriously, however defiant they may sound when such warnings are heard. But so do other countries in the region, whose memories of the brief war with Iraq remain vivid. Yet, the results of U.S. policies are hardly conclusive. Saddam Hussein is still in power, long past the six weeks to six months U.S. President Bush predicted in 1991, and the Shi'ite clergy is still in control in Iran, long after the shah has been forgotten in the West.

Reminders of the Cold War as evidence that containment takes time may seem irresistible but are deceptive.[15] The conditions that made containment work in Europe after World War II were fundamentally different from those in the Gulf after the Cold War. The common interests that shaped the commitment to fight communism and the threat that sustained it, the U.S. power that guaranteed the commitment and the Soviet power that challenged the Western interests do not exist in the case of the Persian Gulf. In 1945, a choice between U.S. president Harry Truman's goodwill and Soviet leader Josef Stalin's good faith was made easy by the tangible benefits (including political stability and economic recovery) provided by the former in contrast to the latter. Moreover, there was a strategy of dual containment in postwar Europe, which consisted of achieving reconciliation with the former enemy (Germany, divided and weak) in order to attend to the emerging confrontation with the former ally (the Soviet Union, united and strong).

Dual containment in the Gulf hardly shows the same degree of interest convergence between the allies, the same measure of Europe's explicit dependence on America's leadership, or the same sustainable commitment of U.S. power to protect Europe's interests. Moreover, irrespective of such conditions, dual containment in the Gulf provides no immediate advantage to Europe. The U.S. strategy appears to require too much time to achieve any result, and progress seems too erratic for many in Europe who find the U.S. containment policy dangerous and self-defeating. They worry about the possible backlash from a demonized Iran, a disintegrating Iraq, and the deteriorating Arab-Israeli peace process. With each side of the Atlantic suspicious of the other's intent and ability to act, there is little room to lead because there is only a limited will to follow. Thus, if Cold War analogies are to be used, they should focus on the link between critical dialogue and dual containment—as was the case during the Cold War when detente was the continuation of containment by other means. Neither Europe nor the United States can escape charges of economic and commercial greed. Every country in Europe wants to be "the Arabs' best friend," but none can guarantee the protection they need to seal that friendship: only the United States can. Although the U.S. ability to guarantee the security of the Arab states is compelling, other goals and commitments in the region make it difficult to translate this guarantee into friendship.

After the Gulf War, the American strategy "to neutralize, contain and, through selective pressures, perhaps eventually transform" such "backlash states" as Iran and Iraq was expected to remain in effect with the active support of the coalition that had waged the war, and "until circumstances change[d]."[16] A change in circumstances was envisioned as a reduced threat from both countries and visibly improving conditions in the whole region. In practice, of course, these assumptions, however justified they may have been after the Gulf War, have not been confirmed.

Arguably, Saddam Hussein will not dare any new adventure for a long time, and the Iranian clergy's inability to govern effectively is eroding their appeal both at home and abroad.[17] Yet, there has been no "dramatic" reduction in the strategic significance of either

Iraq or Iran for Europe. Nor has their impact on U.S.-European relations, or on Western relations with other parts of the world, including other Muslim states and states in Asia, declined significantly. The opposite may well be true.[18] Muslims who look up to the Iranian regime, or to Saddam Hussein's defiance of the West, for inspiration and emulation do not easily accept the sanctions and humiliation imposed on the two countries. This resentment among Muslims is what motivated French foreign minister Hervé de Charette in 1997 to reflect ominously, during a trip in Lebanon, "When violence returns to the Middle East, sooner or later it will show up in Paris."[19]

In addition, the fall in oil prices, which in 1998 reached their lowest level since 1973, points to more, not less, dependence on imported Gulf oil.[20] Demand in the new oil importers of East Asia and South Asia is expected to double by 2015, assuming no new economic upheaval takes place. To a lesser extent this increase in demand will also occur in the United States and Japan. The Gulf states will have nearly to double their current production to help satisfy such increased demand without significant price disruptions.[21] Although their consumption is expected to increase at a more moderate pace of about 8 percent per year, EU states will become even more vulnerable to future instability in the Gulf region than they are today.

Under these circumstances, it is not realistic to expect that the global unity achieved during the Gulf War could last. The U.S. decision to sever all trade and investment relations with Iran on April 30, 1995 was not followed in Europe. On the contrary, the Iran and Libya Sanctions Act (ILSA) that sought to impose sanctions on foreign companies that did business with Iran and Libya made European states close ranks. Even as the Clinton administration debated the desirability of imposing ILSA on the French oil company Total and its partners (Gazprom of Russia and Petronas of Malaysia) in early 1998, Europeans used Tehran's televised opening to the United States as vindication of their call for a critical dialogue. They rely on President Clinton's response of January 27, 1998, as evidence of a willingness to launch a dialogue of his own as well.[22]

In the case of Iraq, an early lift of the UN embargo is not what most EU states want. Still, almost all agree that the embargo may have to be lifted before Saddam Hussein has been removed from power, and most fear a widening backlash against the West not only from Iraqis but from Muslims elsewhere as well. "We do not want there to be a serious destabilization that will add to the problems of this region," stated French defense minister Charles Millon in September 1996, after he refused to associate his country with a U.S. air strike within the internationally recognized borders of northern Iraq.[23] Significantly, it was the Pentagon that announced France's participation in surveillance missions in the "no-fly zone," alongside U.S. and British planes, but it was the French government that announced the end of its participation in these missions in January 1997, on the eve of Deputy Prime Minister Tariq Aziz's third visit to Paris since the Gulf War.

During the prolonged crisis of 1997–98 between Iraq and the United States over the UN weapons inspectors' access to prohibited sites in Iraq, French objections to Clinton's policies expressed European sentiments more convincingly than did British support for these policies.[24] The fact that those objections proved more successful than earlier ones may be an ominous sign of the times, as was the Gulf Cooperation Council (GCC) states' open unwillingness to cooperate during the Western strike against Iraq in September 1996 and the threatened U.S. strikes of March 1998. Barely hidden behind the cover of the UN and its Secretary General Kofi Annan, U.S. isolation grew in 1998. Indeed, notwithstanding the broad diplomatic consensus achieved during another such crisis in November 1998, only Britain joined the United States for yet another strike against Iraq a few weeks later in mid-December—a strike that was launched in spite of the UN rather than in its name.

Finally, the "broader positive trends in the region" that the Clinton administration predicted for the future—not only in the Gulf but also for the Arab-Israeli conflict—have not materialized. In 1991, after the Gulf War and in the aftermath of the Madrid Summit held late that year, the restrictions imposed on Iraq, the then-expected Russian withdrawal as an arms supplier, and Iran's exhaustion as an arms consumer led to the erroneous assumption that the new regional military balance would be kept at lower levels.[25] With Saudi Arabia, Kuwait, and the United Arab Emirates (UAE) weary of security arrangements that proved illusory when exposed to Iraqi aggression in 1990, and with Iran showing renewed concern over its depleted military arsenal, most of the major arms importers today are still from the Middle East. The largest increase in the market share of arms sales in the 1990s has been achieved by the United States and France (at the expense, in part at least, of Britain). There are also new bidders, such as Russia (whose ample arsenal can be lent, leased, or sold) and China, which is in search of new revenues and greater influence abroad.

The deteriorating conditions of the Arab-Israeli peace process, which had been gaining momentum since the 1991 Madrid Summit and the 1993 and 1995 Oslo agreements, have increased the potential for instability in the Middle East. No Arab state could remain indifferent to another collision between Israel and the Palestinians, lest it face charges of collusion with Israel and the United States at a time when most political leaders in the region are aging and losing their once-unquestioned authority. Nor would any European state be likely to remain silent, and their widespread criticism of Israel's intransigence as the main reason for the derailment of a process started (by Europeans) in Oslo might be an especially contentious transatlantic dispute after 1999.

Other reasons for concern abound. In August 1998, for example, a U.S. air strike against Sudan and Afghanistan for their alleged support of a group held responsible for a coordinated attack against the U.S. embassies in Kenya and Tanzania seemed to suggest a more active U.S. policy aimed at any kind of state support for terrorism. If confirmed, such a policy would raise new apprehensions in many countries with a visible U.S. presence that could be the target of future acts of terror, and would increase the levels of tensions between the United States and many Islamic countries. The image of Islam in the United States and other Western countries is harmed further by such other events as the rising levels of dehumanizing killing in Algeria, and the image of the West is harmed further in Islamic countries by a series of decisions that appear to suggest much Western tolerance for the killing of

Muslims (in the Balkans and elsewhere) but much intolerance for any Muslim attempts to acquire means of self-defense (in Pakiştan and elsewhere). Thus, Western and Islamic countries have a good many issues over which to clash, and the United States and the EU states have a good many reasons for disagreement, in the years ahead.

Dialogue and Containment

The U.S. dual containment of Iran and Iraq, enforced despite the resistance of most European states, has run its course. Europe's critical dialogue with Iran, and its selective accommodation of Iraq, pursued despite the U.S. objections, has also run out of steam. The vast majority of the U.S. Congress finds little it likes about Europe's dialogue, but U.S. leadership, however indispensable it may be, can be effective only to the extent that it is followed willingly rather than imposed forcefully. The states of Europe generally welcome an American will to lead, but their will to follow seems to be missing in the absence of certain conditions, namely, a shared vision pointing to collective goals, made plausible by the commitment of sufficient capabilities. The 1998 intervention by the UN Secretary General, which rescued Americans and Europeans from their own divisions but appeared to strengthen Saddam Hussein, demonstrates that the failure to meet these conditions erodes the alliance and strengthens its adversaries.[26] Now, the transatlantic boundaries of permissible differences are tested every time the United States seeks Europe's support for military action and economic sanctions in the Gulf region.

As long as Europe continues to lack a single voice, however, such consultation with the United States on policy toward the Gulf will remain cacophonic. "You have to be a genius or French to understand Europe,"[27] reportedly observed Secretary of State Madeleine Albright as the 1998 crisis over Iraq was coming to a head. Notwithstanding the scarcity of "geniuses" able to understand the French, France can still speak on behalf of Europe, which it can "understand," according to Secretary Albright at least. "In the Middle East," declared Foreign Minister Hervé de Charette in early 1996, "we are still able to shape history."[28] Such claims are hardly enough to assert France as America's European interlocutor in the region, however. Indeed, France's attempt to be such an interlocutor can be effective only as long as French leverage with Germany is high, Germany's resistance to pulling its weight in Europe is deep, and Europe's distance from Britain is wide. That all these conditions are changing does not augur well for France's claim to EU leadership in coming years.

Great Britain, as the former hegemon in the Gulf and the most dependable U.S. ally, is the other European state that can help set the terms of U.S.-European and intra-European consultation in the Gulf region. Its role as a credible broker between the United States and Europe, and within Europe, can be based on Britain's growing influence across the Channel and on its renewed influence across the Atlantic. The constructive ambiguities of this emerging role were demonstrated in early 1998, when Britain's alignment with the United States on Iraq helped balance France's opposition to U.S. policy and Germany's passive acquiescence. In the spring, British Foreign Secretary Robin Cook traveled to the Middle East, where his provocative statements on Israel helped balance an allegedly more cooperative attempt by the United States to relaunch the Arab-Israeli peace process and protect Israel from the political isolation that was about to engulf it.

More transatlantic discord over the Gulf in 1999, whether caused by the evidence of failure or by a sense of insufficient consultation (before decisions are made) or cooperation (after they are enforced), could seriously disrupt U.S.-European relations and affect the vital interests of all the Western allies. What is at issue is not U.S. military power, but when, how, where, why, with whom, against whom, and to what ends such power is or might be used. The United States and the states of Europe, and the two institutions they built together (NATO and the EU), are needed to enforce a comprehensive strategy that can rely on credible military deterrence and convincing economic inducements. The problems raised by Iran and Iraq are too diverse for their resolution to be enclosed in a single formula. Dual containment and constructive dialogue explain neither what is to be contained specifically (and how) nor what is to be discussed explicitly (and to what end).

Issues of economic growth, demographic explosion, political governance, cultural coexistence, and many other topics are left unexplored.

More generally, a process of transatlantic policy coordination could involve a small core group of states that belong to NATO and the European Union and that would draft common policies for consideration by all the EU and NATO partners. The procedure could resemble the *directoire* of Western powers France proposed in the past. (That the idea was at best premature then does not make it wrong now.) Although this is not the place to define the specific features of such a dialogue, it is important to point to some of the leading questions that it should address. The most significant are finding a common policy to deny Iraq access to chemical and biological weapons; isolating Saddam Hussein whenever his actions threaten to disrupt the regional environment (by swift and decisive military action if necessary); and destabilizing (and, ultimately, overthrowing) his regime by extending support for an Iraqi opposition and assisting nongovernmental organizations to help the general populace with additional assistance, which could come out of the Iraqi assets currently frozen in the United States and elsewhere.

In the case of Iran, the transatlantic dialogue would have to agree first of all on the desirability of an immediate opening to Iran, both as part of a coherent strategy against Iraq as well as on its own merits—on the basis of the agenda of common concerns that has been discussed with Iran many times in the past few years. Admittedly, as this agenda is addressed, the process of normalization with Iran will take time, which should be a good reason for starting earlier rather than later. Such a strategy could entail loosening the visa policy toward citizens from Iran and unfreezing some of the Iranian assets in the United States. These first steps in turn would help convince Tehran of the U.S. intent to eventually normalize relations without compromising on the serious issues that divide both countries. That policy would dilute the U.S. threat of sanctions against foreign firms and help convince Europeans of the U.S. determination to work with Europe without compromising its interests in the Gulf.

A Euro-American dialogue on the Persian Gulf might mean a more moderate rhetoric vis-à-vis adversaries, but it will also require a softer rhetoric vis-à-vis allies. Although the states of Europe may not be indispensable to the solution of the problems in the Gulf region, neither are they a central part of these problems. A Euro-American dialogue on the Gulf would not end transatlantic and intra-European economic rivalries throughout these areas. Such a dialogue would presuppose, however, that in most instances transatlantic cooperation is more likely to succeed, and disagreements less likely to escalate, if preceded by genuine consultation before decisions are made. U.S. and European interests in the Gulf are too important for one side not to know what the other side is doing, or for one side to expect the other to follow its leadership unquestioningly.

Notes

1. Robert Blackwill and Michael Stürmer, *Allies Divided, Transatlantic Policies for the Greater Middle East* (Cambridge, Mass.: MIT Press, 1997), 1.

2. F. Gregory Gause, "The Illogic of Dual Containment," *Foreign Affairs* 73, no. 2 (March-April 1994): 58; and Stephen Zunes, "Hazardous Hegemony: The United States in the Middle East," *Current History* 96, no. 606 (January 1997): 20–24.

3. Stanley Hoffmann, "La France, les Etats-Unis et le conflit israélo-arabe: Différences et asymétries, 1967–1971" (France, the United States, and the Arab-Israeli conflict: differences and asymmetries), *Politique Etrangère* 36, no. 1: 659.

4. Kenneth Stein, "Will Europe and America Ever Agree?" *Middle East Quarterly* 4, no. 1 (March 1997): 39. Hussein J. Agha, "The Middle East and Europe: The Post-Cold War Climate," in Hugh Miall, ed., *Redefining Europe: New Patterns of Conflict and Cooperation* (London: Royal Institute of International Affairs, 1996), 249. Shireen T. Hunter, *The Future of Islam and the West: Clash of Civilizations or Peaceful Coexistence?* (Westport, Conn.: Praeger, 1998), 169.

5. François Heisbourg, "Population Movements in Post-Cold War Europe," *Survival* 33, no. 1 (January-February 1991); Alec Hargraves and Timothy Stenhouse, "The Gulf War and the Maghrebian Community in France," *Maghreb Review* 17, no. 1/2, (1992): 44; B. A. Robertson, "Islam and Europe: An Enigma or a Myth," *Middle East Journal* 48, no. 2 (Spring 1994): 302.

6. Patrick Clawson, *Business as Usual? Western Policy Options Toward Iran, International Perspectives* 33 (September 1995), 3; Patrick Clawson, "What to do about Iran," Middle East Quarterly 2, no. 4 (December 1995): 39–49.

7. *The Middle East and North Africa* (London: Europa Publications, 1998), 483 and 535. International Monetary Fund, *International Statistical Yearbook*, vol. 18 (1995), pp. 448–451.

8. For example, Mouna Naim, "Les pressions s'accentuent pour la levée des sanctions contre l'Iraq" (Pressures are building to lift sanctions against Iraq), *Le Monde*, January 12, 1996.

9. Agis Salpukas, "Conoco Signs Contract with Iran to Develop Persian Gulf Oilfield," *New York Times*, March 7, 1995.

10. Rolf Ekéus, "Dismantling Saddam's Arsenal," *Middle East Quarterly* 3, no. 1 (March 1996): 71–76. Joachim Krause, "The Proliferation of Weapons of Mass Destruction: The Risks for Europe," in Paul Cornish, Peter van Ham, and Joachim Krause, *Europe and the Challenge of Proliferation*, Chaillot Papers, no. 24 (Paris: WEU Institute for Security Studies, 1996), 7.

11. Televised interview, March 13, 1996, "The Charm El Chiekh Summit," with Jean-Claude Narcy (TF-1) and Daniel Bilalian (France-2).

12. Robert Deutsch, "US Sanctions against Iran at Center Stage," *The Oil and Gas Journal* 94, no. 23 (June 1996): 28; and James Woolsey, "Appeasement will only encourage Iran," *Survival* 38, no. 4 (Winter 1996–97): 18.

13. Klaus Kinkel's interview was reported in *Foreign Broadcast Information Service* (FBIS), Western Europe, April 14, 1997.

14. The evidence of Iran's involvement had been available for many years. "Behind all these crimes stands a sovereign state. . . . Iran . . .," concluded a 1993 investigation of the German Federal Crime Office, quoted in a *Washington Post* report on "The Killing of Iranian Dissenters: Bloody Trail Back to Tehran," November 21, 1993. Cited in Clawson, *Business as Usual? Western Policy Toward Iran*, p. 16.

15. Peter Rodman, "Why Ease Up on Iran?" *Washington Post*, December 11, 1996.

16. Anthony Lake, "Confronting the Backlash States," *Foreign Affairs* 173, no. 2 (March/April 1994); also, Martin Indyck, "The Clinton Administration's Approach to the Middle East," Washington Institute for Near East Policy, Washington, DC, May 18, 1993.

17. Robin Wright, "Dateline Tehran: Revolution Imploding," *Foreign Policy*, no. 103 (Summer 1996); Olivier Roy, "Faut-il diaboliser l'Iran?" (Should we demonize Iran?), *Politique Internationale*, no. 78 (Winter 1997–1998): 358, and "Téhéran: le poids des armes" (Tehran: The weight of arms), *Politique Internationale*, no. 60 (Summer 1993): 273.

18. Zbigniew Brzezinski, Brent Scowcroft, and Richard Murphy, "Differentiated Containment," *Foreign Affairs* 76, no. 3 (May/June 1997): 27; Harvey Sicherman, "The Strange Death of Dual Containment," *Orbis* 41, no. 2 (Spring 1997): 223–240.

19. Interview by Marie-Laure Cittanova, *Les Echos* (Paris), April 8, 1997, p. 4. Concerns about home-grown disorders were reportedly part of French President François Mitterrand's attempts to avoid war in January 1991. In Algeria, the war proved to be a catalyst for disorders whose impact was soon to be uncovered.

20. Zalmay Khalilzad, "The United States and the Persian Gulf: Preventing Regional Hegemony," *Survival* 37, no. 2 (Summer 1995): 96.

21. The demand increase will be steeper if Russia and the former Soviet republics develop more quickly than is currently expected. Geoffrey Kemp, *Energy Superbowl: Strategic Politics and the Persian Gulf and Caspian Basin*, (Washington, D.C.: Nixon Center for Peace and Freedom, 1997), 4. C. William Maynes, "The Middle East in the Twenty-First Century," *Middle East Journal* 52, no. 1 (Winter 1998): 15.

22. For a discussion of these events, see Gary Sick, "Rethinking Dual Containment," *Survival* 40, no. 1 (Spring 1998): 5–32, and Patrick Clawson, "The Continuing Logic of Dual Containment," Ibid., 33–47.

23. Interview by Jacques-Marie Bourget, *Paris-Match*, September 5, 1996, pp. 56–57.

24. In early 1998, the French in particular were jubilant. See, for example, Jean-Marie Colombani in *Le Monde*, February 26, 1998, and Alain Peyrefitte in *Le Figaro*, February 24, 1998, as well as Jean Daniel in *Le Nouvel Observateur*, February 26, 1998, and Claude Imbert in *Le Point*, February 27, 1998. Most French observers agreed that France had played a decisive role during the crisis, vis-à-vis the United States (Daniel and Imbert) or in spite of its objections (Colombani and Peyrefitte).

25. Between 1986 and 1992, Iran's defense spending relative to total government expenditures fell from 55.2 to 24.9 percent. For the period 1992-95, Saudi Arabia concluded agreements worth $22.3 billion, which is 80 percent of all purchases made by Iran, Kuwait, UAE, Egypt, and Israel (ranked third, and fifth through eighth worldwide in defense spending relative to total expenditures). The U.S. share of arms sales amounted to 56.4 percent (compared to a 40.3 percent share in 1988-1991) while the French share was 26.6 percent (compared to 4.8 percent during the previous period). Richard Grimmett, *Conventional Arms Transfers to Developing Nations, 1988–1995*, Washington, D.C.: Congressional Research Service, August 15, 1996, pp. 48–50. Also, U.S. Arms Control and Disarmament Agency, *World Military Expenditures and Arms Transfers* (Washington D.C.: Government Printing Office, 1995), p. 12, and Hasan Johar and Gawdat Bahgar, "The

American Dilemma in the Gulf Region," *Journal of South Asian and Middle Eastern Studies* 19, no. 1 (Fall 1995): 61.

26. Andrew Fenton Cooper, Richard A. Higgott, Kim Richard Nossal, "Bound to Follow? Leadership and Followership in the Gulf Conflict," *Political Science Quarterly* 106, no. 3 (1991): 408. Henry Kissinger, "Our Shilly-Shally 'Strategy' on Saddam," *Washington Post*, March 23, 1998.

27. "Cacophonie européenne" (European cacophony), *Le Monde*, February 11, 1998, p. 14.

28. Interview, *Paris Match*, May 2, 1996; also, *L'Express*, April 25, 1996. De Charette's successor, Hubert Védrine has been more realistic as he has tried to overcome, in his own words, France's "difficulty [in] placing itself in relation to world reality." Quoted in a Reuters news report, October 8, 1997, no. 1446.

7

Memories of Leadership

THERE HAVE BEEN MOMENTS IN HISTORY when America led because of what it did and how effectively it did it, rather than because of what it said and how forcefully it said it. The aftermath of World War II was such a moment. The vision shaped the policies, although, admittedly, the policies eventually changed the vision. Neither the vision nor the policies were welcomed readily, at home or abroad, and neither was enforced easily, then or in subsequent years. Altogether, the ever-more ambitious goals attached to an increasingly global vision proved to be significantly more costly and painful than had been anticipated. But in the end, the policies worked and the vision was fulfilled, to America's benefit as well as to the benefit of others.

The Way to Lead

The postwar leadership expected from President Truman and his administration was demanding. The United States had to be, and was, decisive and assertive. Memories of what had been done in 1919, and not done in 1939, lingered. Europe was too important to be left to the Europeans and their failed diplomatic maneuvers. Decisions would have to come from the United States, and in the United States they would have to be made at the top—when announcing a doctrine that carried the president's name or an aid program that bore the name of the heroic secretary of state. The foreign policy men surrounding Truman were all leaders in their own right: they stood where they did because of what they had achieved in the past, and they acted as they did because of what they believed about the future. Yet, even as the best and the brightest of their time, they remained the president's men. Challenges to the president's power carried a price, as then-secretary of state James

Byrnes learned in early 1947, and so did the evidence of failure, as General Douglas MacArthur also learned three years later after his disastrous decision to bring the Korean War closer to China.

The Truman leadership was also bold and innovative. Its ability to think anew about American foreign policy took it away from both U.S. traditions and established patterns of international relations. Thus, when devising the mechanics of Europe's economic recovery and the dynamics of its political reconciliation, the United States turned its back on the nation's history of disentanglement from Europe and launched policies that were to force the nations of Europe to change the course of their own history. At the same time, these policies of reconstruction and reconciliation were preempting the distant memories of George Washington's bid for distance from the quagmire of Europe during the Napoleonic wars, and George Clémenceau's bid for revenge on Germany after World War I.

Boldness and innovation also made these policies generous, but generosity was not extended to such a point as to deny America's self-interests. Reading the early critics who complained of the administration's "idealism" illustrates the shortcomings of theorists and pundits. When ending the war in the Pacific with two atomic bombs, drawing the line in Europe and Asia with unprecedented peacetime commitments, or joining the fray in the former European empires, the Truman administration rarely lost sight of the nation's interests. How ironic it is that it was up to the next school of revisionist historians to unveil, one generation later, the reality of the U.S. concern with its national interests.[1] Who dares think what the world might be like today had the United States not been willing to make the needed commitments and provide the indispensable leadership—at least to and for those parts of the world that mattered most to the United States? When agreeing to unprecedented levels of aid to Europe, when providing that aid in the form of grants, when linking these grants to the development of cooperative institutions, the United States became committed to a redistribution of its power and, by implication, its influence as well. When making the security of many European states, and later, many states in Asia, an American responsibility, when making that responsibility credible with a nearly unlimited deployment of ground forces, and when allowing these forces to engage in costly wars whose bad memories still linger in the nation's psyche, U.S. leadership exposed the absurdity of those who had thought that American power could not be trusted because the will to endure the pain it caused could not last.

Although the general public hardly showed interest in, or comprehension for, initiatives that were introduced at a quick pace between 1947 and 1951, the persistently "new" Truman administration kept these initiatives sufficiently integrated to make the vision comprehensive. No policy, however bold it might be, and no crisis, however revolutionary it might seem, could hijack the policy debate long enough to derail further decisions on other issues. The Truman leadership relied on economic, political, and military instruments to combine institution building and bilateral relations as the two sides of the same security coin and understood the connectedness of developments in Asia and developments in Europe.

Finally, even as U.S. postwar leadership proved to be domineering when imposing its will on others, it remained flexible when necessary. That the Truman vision would have seemed as erratic as it was for so many years was due, in part at least, to the adjustments that were made along the way. These adjustments included fighting a land war in Asia whose prospect it had dismissed earlier as sheer folly, but respecting the constraints that could keep the war limited (also a new concept in American history at the time); developing an integrated military organization with its European allies, which made a sustained and substantial deployment of U.S. forces in Europe inevitable, notwithstanding earlier pledges to the contrary; and even giving containment the global dimension that it had been explicitly designed to eschew when first launched.

Over time, the qualities showed by such U.S. leadership produced the policies and devised the architecture out of which victory ensued. Allies accepted these policies and moved into that architecture (or resisted the temptation to move into alternative structures) because they believed in the full range of commitments that were made by the United States to their recovery and security. In other words, there was a point for other states to follow U.S. leadership because there was a shared appreciation of its end points. Adversaries, too, respected U.S. leadership, including a continued

U.S. presence in Europe and a growing involvement elsewhere, because they respected the totality of the U.S. power that underlined them, even when they deeply disapproved of the manner in which such power was used or denied. In short, there was considerable power behind the U.S. commitment to containment, and there was a common will to use such power if the boundaries of permissible behavior were ignored by the Soviet Union or any other state; there was a vision behind containment, and there was a shared ability to enforce elements of that vision on the Western side of the line containment had drawn.

These memories need not carry a tone of triumphalism over what was achieved and seems to have been forgotten, but they can convey a sense of nostalgia over what used to be but seems to be no more. That William Jefferson Clinton is no Harry S. Truman reflects more than the personal differences and experiences between the two men. No less, and possibly more, significant are the differences that separate the nation (and its people) over which Clinton presides after the Cold War, relative to the nation (and its people) his distant predecessor inherited after World War II. These differences include the changed structural conditions of a world in which U.S. power is without peer and without immediate challenger, and the role of institutions that now regulate the behavior of nation-states whose sovereignty has been eroded steadily as a consequences of membership.[2]

No Will to Follow

The overwhelming amount of power accumulated by the United States since World War II and the quality of its leadership during the Cold War were displayed most impressively during the Gulf War in January 1991. Since that time, when the world was first exposed to the unipolar consequences of the Soviet collapse, there have been few moments of U.S. activism in the world.

One such moment occurred during the three-month transition that followed President George Bush's loss in the presidential elections of November 1992. Traditionally, these transitions demand a will for abstinence from the outgoing president and pleas of continuity from the president-elect. Departures from this tradition have been not only rare but ineffective. Thus, in 1968, President Lyndon Johnson's desire to begin talks on strategic arms limitations was motivated by his consuming eagerness to leave office with some global statement of hope. Only the Soviet invasion of Czechoslovakia aborted the then-scheduled summit meeting of September 30, 1968 with Soviet Premier Alexei Kosygin. After the election, however, Richard Nixon's strong objections to any U.S.-Soviet summit before his inauguration were communicated explicitly in Washington as well as in Moscow, and ended both Johnson's efforts and Kosygin's responsiveness. As compensation of sort, Johnson was later "authorized" to urge the South Vietnamese government in Saigon to accept an offer of compromise with the government in Hanoi before his departure from office on January 20, 1969, on the explicit understanding that such an offer was "meaningless" anyway.[3] Eight years later, in November 1976, Henry Kissinger seemed to remember these conditions as he did nothing during the transition to Jimmy Carter that might be seen as distracting from, or obstructing, the "high expectations and ambitious goals" that surrounded the new president's hopes for a new beginning.[4]

In November 1992, however, George Bush showed little inhibition. Had there been any complaints from the president-elect, the outgoing president and his advisers would have simply ignored them. Bush's apparent determination to make last-minute foreign policy decisions was probably motivated by his deep personal conviction that Clinton was, and would remain, unable to understand the world, let alone manage it, with the same effectiveness as Bush knew he could and most Americans agreed he had. Accordingly, Bush spent his last weeks in office trying to hedge against future policy reversals and errors by imposing on the president-elect decisions that he made and even began to enforce on his behalf.

Thus, the votes had barely been counted when Bush was ending the time-out which he had taken from the world during the previous 12 months: deploying U.S. forces in Somalia to fight against starvation at last; signing a trade pact with Canada and Mexico; escalating a trade conflict over farm issues with the European allies to pressure them into a quicker agreement on the then-ongoing round of trade negotiations; going to Moscow in order to sign an agreement for deep missile cuts; sending a flotilla near Haiti, mainly to control the flow of refugees to Florida; raising the tone over Bosnia, but avoiding any tangible action; tightening the arms ban on Iran and striking at Iraq on several occasions, up to the very last day of January 20, 1993, as a (bitter?) farewell message to a defiant (and gloating?) Saddam Hussein.[5] Over these and many other issues, and in a variety of international forums, Bush defined his successor's foreign policy agenda and constrained many of the decisions that Clinton was to make in 1993.

A second burst of U.S. activism occurred in 1995. After the new Republican majority in Congress had denied President Clinton sufficient political space at home, Clinton sought relief abroad. Where else could the president still gain bipartisan support in Congress and public applause throughout the country? The world gave the politically embattled president the stage he needed for the many roles he performed abroad: appropriately somber when threatening foes that offend America's civility and threaten U.S. interests, convincingly joyful when endorsing peace initiatives that would save children from ongoing or future wars, and historically mature when welcoming at the White House former rogue leaders now willing to proclaim their intention to change their ways.

In so doing, the president developed his foreign policy agenda as he had earlier masterminded his domestic agenda: at home, one majority per issue and one issue per majority; abroad, a commitment for each crisis but only one crisis for each commitment. Wherever there was ground for asserting ownership of an initiative launched by others (with the Arab-Israeli peace process developed in Oslo) or for launching an initiative of his own (most notably on Northern Ireland), Clinton moved quickly and spoke eloquently. Examples included the peace he envisioned for the Middle East, the fiery speech that won him deafening applause in Dublin, the few tears shed over Rwanda between two planes, a few (and increasingly customary) Stinger missiles against Iraq, a dialogue with Russia or China that could be equally defiant or conciliatory, and a bit of lecturing about good governments south of the border or about sound economic management across the Pacific. There were many trips, especially in Europe where he could enter history through the back door of his predecessors' achievements, from the fiftieth anniversary of the landing in Normandy, symbolically spent in May 1994 at Omaha Beach (and less appropriately in Moscow as well), through the fiftieth anniversary of the Marshall Plan (spent near Maastricht in the Netherlands, where he could also connect with the aspirations of European unity signed into a treaty six years earlier), to the fiftieth anniversary of the 1949 North Atlantic Treaty for NATO enlargement as a prologue to America's grand historical farewell to the twentieth century.

This approach worked. In 1996, the statesmanship Clinton's initiatives seemed to display in the world helped restore his image in the United States. Throughout, however, these initiatives all suffered from the same disturbing flaw: they entailed a commitment that was made without a clear explanation of the interests that should have motivated them, and, no less important, without an appreciation of the capabilities needed to enforce them. The tempting "distraction" that was passing for leadership was the shoving and cajoling of allies and adversaries alike over small and large issues alike. In time, however, the temptation could prove fatal. With no opportunity too small to be ignored, no commitment might be deemed too big to avoid. What passes for commitments and is praised as leadership is the illusion that new friendships can be built at no cost and that enemies can be defeated without tears.

Clinton's management of Bosnia in the context of NATO and its enlargement is a case in point. As the Cold War was ending in 1989–1991, NATO started a remarkable transformation that showed an institutional will for changes in strategy, structure, and missions. These changes, however, were not designed to produce a "new" security structure but to confirm the old structure, however adapted it would have to be to accommodate the new geopolitical era. In 1991, these adaptations were to be engineered by the United States with, and on behalf of, the allies. In 1993, Clinton was more sensitive to Europe's will to play an expanded role of its own, and the adaptation of NATO was to be completed, therefore, by the allies with the United States. Only after the war in Bosnia had confirmed the inability of the states of Europe to do as much as they had intended, did the United States revert to doing as much as Bush had envisioned in early 1991, which was certainly more than Clinton had wanted in early 1993. Thus, the "lessons" taught in Bosnia and elsewhere were lessons that had been learned before, but were conveniently forgotten or deceptively ignored by the new democratic administration: first, that the continued unavailability of European power made American power indispensable and, second, that the persistent centrality of U.S. leadership made NATO central as well, because NATO was the only multilateral conduit to Europe for both U.S. power and U.S. leadership.

With Europe bitterly weary of the U.S. refusal to help on the ground in Bosnia, while criticizing the effectiveness of Europe's own military action; with the United States openly leery of the compromise the Europeans were trying to negotiate over a unitary state in Bosnia, without offering an alternative plan it could call its own; and with the Europeans wary of the historical reflexes that some of them were displaying anew in the Balkans, there was much cause for concern over the future course of transatlantic relations and the future of stability in Europe. In 1995, therefore, the strategic goal of the Clinton administration in the Balkans was not only to end the war and save Bosnia but also to save Europe and even the United States from themselves—the former's tragic history of bloody conflicts and failed resolve, and the latter's foolish history of isolation and self-denial.

How President Clinton addressed these daunting goals is revealing: following a small dinner held for French President Jacques Chirac, the president, according to Richard Holbrooke's candid account, learned of a "bold and dangerous plan" that included the use of 20,000 U.S. troops in Bosnia with serious risks of significant casualties. "Is this true?" Clinton reportedly asked Secretary of State Warren Christopher in apparent disbelief.[6]

So it was, then, that Clinton came to reappraise his policy in Bosnia, the policy on which depended the value and durability of other postwar achievements in Europe but one the U.S. president adopted only as the better of two bad and unwanted options. The goal to which he had committed U.S. power would have been no better than the moral equivalent of surrender because it would have been designed to provide military cover for a withdrawal, under duress, from an ongoing war. But the refusal to act in the face of the allies' request would have been no less than the diplomatic equivalent of betrayal, because of Clinton's earlier commitment that U.S. forces would be made available for the extraction of UN forces from Bosnia, if and when needed. After incredulous publics on both sides of the Atlantic had watched retreating Western forces harassed by Serbs, Croats, and even Bosnians—with or without American involvement—how much support would have been left for NATO and for a central U.S. role in Europe? If there could be no public support in the United States for use of American power in Europe, how could there be support for a U.S. role elsewhere?

The exercise of world leadership will require more experience, more interest, more will, more explanations, and more credibility from the U.S. president to forge the flexible coalitions needed to face the unforeseeable crises that loom ahead. But calls for flexibility can be heard too easily as warnings of unpredictability, what is unforeseen often results from a lack of foresight, and what passes for hindsight often reflects an erosion of national will and alliance cohesion. With both the American public and the allies openly supportive of U.S. policies if, or as soon as, they have worked, the main criterion of followership is not leadership, whatever the vision that animates it, but the perception of success, however durable it may be. With victory as a precondition for action, the temptation to postpone decisions indefinitely may be irresistible because every option will always face a large group of skeptics who can block it from their respective capitals or from NATO and the EU or United Nations, or compromise it with deceptive exit strategies designed to pledge success by a given time, or end it abruptly with the first sight of American casualties or allies' unreliability.

The irony is that, in the end, the neglect, the confusion, and the improvisations that characterized U.S. decisions in the Balkans up to 1995 ensured, beyond Bosnia, the resurrection of U.S. leadership and the centrality of American power for the new security arrangements in Europe. Having thus "saved" NATO and whatever remained of Bosnia in Dayton, Holbrooke could turn to enlarging the Western alliance in order to protect old and new members alike from further Bosnias elsewhere.

"No issue," noted Holbrooke, "has been more important, controversial or misunderstood than whether NATO should remain an alliance of its 16 current members or expand, and if it expands, why, where, when and how."[7] Not the least reason behind such public misunderstanding was that the two questions that should have been raised first—why and how—were addressed only after the two questions that should have been raised last had already been answered: where (in Central Europe, which included Poland but pointedly excluded any of the former Soviet states whose membership in NATO might be most offensive to Russia) and when (in April 1999, when the president could thus make a blind date with history).[8] To delay or deny membership for the countries of Central Europe after enlargement had been pledged unequivocally would have verged on irresponsibility because it would have endangered an organization that most acknowledged as essential to stability in Europe. The criteria for membership, endorsed by all 16 NATO members in December 1995, therefore justified a political decision rather than defined a strategic choice. Even on the eve of the ratification debate in the U.S. Senate, the President would still not tell why and how enlargement was to take place: his 1998 State of the Union Message gave NATO only 92 banal and inconsequential words. In February 1998, shortly before the Senate vote for ratification, which fewer than 20 Senators were prepared to oppose, 61 percent of the American public approved of enlargement even though 68 percent admitted no or little knowledge of what enlargement was all about.[9]

In the end, enlargement from 16 to 19 members came to rest on a logic deemed so self-evident as to require no explanation: expand or disband. Pointedly, therefore, the logic of enlargement from 16 to 19 members can also be used to justify a pause before any further enlargement beyond 19. The arguments are the same: concern over Russia's reaction, which conditioned the initial choice of the new members, but can now stand in the way of other members in former Soviet territories to which Moscow would be more sensitive; the pace of Europe's own expansion, which had left NATO with no alternative to stepping up its own enlargement but could justify a delay after 1999 (pending Europe's own expansion to 20 members around the year 2003); and the state of domestic support, which favored enlargement from 16 to 19 members but might turn against additional expansion should the costs, financial and human, prove to be more demanding than predicted.

The ambiguity Clinton cultivated before 1997 will lose its constructive qualities after 1999, when countries from the Baltics to the Balkans complain of the gloomy future they fear in the absence of NATO membership. To bring in one of the Balkan states (like Slovenia) without any of the Baltic states would be viewed as conceding to a weak and divided Russia a right of veto over NATO decisions that Moscow did not have when the Soviet Union was strong and seemingly united. However, to bring in one of the Baltic states (like Lithuania) without a country such as Romania (or even Bulgaria) would be to worsen its isolation because EU membership for these countries is unlikely to come for many years. To bring in the Baltic states, Slovenia and Romania, as well as Slovakia and Bulgaria, might deny NATO the cohesion it would need all the more explicitly as Russia's future response would itself remain unclear for the near future.

The Persian Gulf represents yet another demonstration of a U.S. failure of will and vision. Initially, the policy of dual containment was an elegant adjustment to the domestic needs faced by the new president. In opposition to Jimmy Carter, President Ronald Reagan's firmness toward Iran had colored a revived American image in the world until the so-called contra scandal had tarnished both the president's and the nation's image during the waning days of the Reagan administration. Notwithstanding Reagan's accommodation of Iraq during and after its war with Iran, President Bush's will for war with Iraq when its armies invaded Kuwait, and his firmness after the end of the war, had also helped confirm U.S. primacy in the world. Such unconditional opposition to the ayatollahs and to Saddam Hussein could not be changed by a young Democratic president who knew little of the world and its odd ways. These states had at their helm rogue regimes whose demise was an unnegotiable prerequisite to a public willingness to accept a change in U.S. policies toward either. Thus evolved the rationale of "dual containment"—a rationale which could neither suggest a geopolitical vision nor permit an effective political leadership.

As a geopolitical vision, dual containment assumed that the Persian Gulf would become both less important and less dangerous; that Western and Gulf countries would remain willing to accept U.S. leadership; and that broader trends in the region and its immediate neighborhood would continue to improve. In practice, these assumptions proved to be wrong as they progressively lost whatever justification they had after the Gulf War.[10] Saddam, explained Clinton relentlessly, is one of the leading "predators of the twenty-first century."[11] He breaks his promises, Clinton added at the Pentagon on February 17, 1998, does not play by the rules, makes false declarations, imposes "debilitating conditions" on United Nations inspectors who try to do their jobs, and lives lavishly in oversized palaces. It was almost as an afterthought that the president reminded his audience that Saddam also builds a lot of dangerous chemical and biological weapons at great cost. Even the president's warning that Saddam will use his arsenal for sure in the future could be heard almost as an afterthought, and the U.S. goal was no more than to weaken him "seriously" and, should that not be enough, to "be prepared to strike him again" seriously, but always later and never decisively.

With many of the allies suspicious of the United States' goals—its willingness to explain what it does and its ability to execute what it says—there is limited will for followership because there is little understanding of the proposed leadership. Thus, in early 1998, several months of U.S. diplomacy designed to convince Saddam "that the international community has [not] lost its will" could convince only a few nations of the American intent, relative to both the 1991 coalition and the reality of the threat—the United Kingdom, Germany, Spain and Portugal, Denmark and the Netherlands, Hungary and Poland and the Czech Republic, Argentina, Iceland, Australia, New Zealand, and Canada. In the future, a U.S. veto may be required to deny a resolution of the UN Security Council aimed at lifting the sanctions imposed upon Baghdad.

A Certain Air of Destiny

Clinton's hopes to gain a place in history came naturally in the area of domestic policies. Notwithstanding some serious misgiving about his personal conduct, the public responsiveness to the president's leadership has been shown often and confirmed repeatedly. His flair for leadership is not, however, nearly as spontaneous in the area of foreign policy. There, the discomfort Clinton still feels is always apparent. Speeches prepared by his advisers are read careful-ly, as Clinton laboriously gives his voice the right tone and his stare the right look. George Kennan, who knows a lot about leadership and visions, put it well many years ago when he wrote of leaders who ask "not: how effective what I am doing [is] in terms of the impact it makes on our world . . . but rather: how do I look, in the mirror of domestic opinion, as I do it? Do I look shrewd, deter-mined, defiantly patriotic, imbued with the necessary vigilance. . . ? If so, this is what I do, even though it may prove to be meaningless, or even counterproductive . . ."[12]

Henry Kissinger, too, knows a lot about leadership and visions. The words he wrote about President Johnson apply well to President Clinton: "one never had the impression that he would think about the topic spontaneously—while shaving, for example."[13] The skills Clinton displayed when attending to his domestic agenda—a sense of timing, a responsiveness to compro-mises based on a knack for multiple convictions, a will for consul-tation based on a passion for diversity, an open predilection for the feasible over the ideal—are not suited as well for foreign policy, about which his interest, rather episodic, takes the form of a trans-fer of his practices from the domestic to the foreign arenas. So it was, for example, when Clinton chose to dispatch his national security team to a town meeting in Ohio in order to explain the then-imminent U.S. strike against Iraq, in late February 1998. What works for a political battle with the Republican Party over the budget and even trade policy, when money and jobs are at stake, does not work as effectively for diplomacy and war, which often deal with life-and-death issues.

All too often, it now seems, the rhetoric drives the commit-ment, the commitment shapes the action, and the action is occa-sionally made to fit into a vision. No wonder, then, if nearly a decade after the end of the Cold War, a world in awe of American power, economic as well as military, has been growing restless with a U.S. leadership that is questioned as intrusive, hazardous, decep-tive, and unreliable: intrusive because of hegemonic tendencies that have been especially evident since Dayton; hazardous because the cost of U.S. policies and the price of its failures must often be borne by other states; deceptive because of a U.S. tendency to rely on ideals to hide its self-interests; and unreliable because of its dependence on constitutional and even historical guidelines that are not fully understandable abroad.

A vision grows out of what is praised before anything has failed, but it is remembered after everything that failed has been forgotten: it is the latter evidence of success, therefore, that defines a vision worth adopting and, conversely, it is the subsequent realities of failure that make it worthless. Praises for the Truman Doctrine as the visionary setting of containment, after World War II and during the Cold War, were more emphatic in 1948 (the year of the Czech coup and the Berlin blockade) and in 1988 (when Mikhail Gorbachev was paving the way for the revolutions in the East) than in 1968 (the year of Vietnam, from the swamps of Southeast Asia to the streets of Chicago) or in 1980 (the year when a window of American vulnerability seemed to have been opened wide to an increasingly hostile and dangerous world). With the understanding that the evidence of success comes slowly and must be accumulated over time, a leadership worthy of being followed is one that is not only viewed as necessary now but is also deemed to be sustainable over time. Although 50 years of cold war should have confirmed America's staying power once and for all, the future of America's role in the world continues to be debated around the two poles of complete withdrawal and global engagement, as if there could ever be a choice between either of these extremes.

At half-past-Clinton, the U.S. administration has had a few tactical successes that, as was the case in 1991 at half-past-Bush, often deserved more credit than they received. In 1998, the world seemed safer and more responsive to U.S. interests and influence than was the case in 1993 (or at any other time during the Cold War and during the inter-war years). Throughout, warnings from critics and pundits alike have proven wrong more often than not. Russia learned to live with NATO enlargement to the countries of Central Europe, and so did the U.S. Senate, notwithstanding earlier warnings that Russia would rebel, the Senate would object, and the public would defect. Peace still prevails in Bosnia, and the philosophy of a unitary state that conditioned the Dayton agreements has withstood the test of time without the casualties that were anticipated in large numbers. The bailout in Mexico worked, U.S.

corporate mergers challenged by the European Commission have not derailed U.S.-EU relations (as was feared briefly in 1997 with the Boeing-McDonnell merger), the financial crisis in Asia caused no global meltdown, and a common European currency was launched on time and without any turbulent impact on exchange rates and the role of the U.S. dollar.

From the Gulf to the Caribbean, the likes of the ayatollahs, Saddam Hussein, and Fidel Castro are still in power, to be sure. Yet, Iran's language has turned less hostile and its demeanor is opening the door to a constructive dialogue with the United States to which Clinton is responding. The effective containment of Saddam Hussein keeps him in a small cage, out of which his occasional barks lack the military bite they used to have to force an explosion there even if they continue to disrupt U.S. relations with the allies there and elsewhere. As to Castro, time, which has become his main obstacle to staying the course, has also turned into America's most reliable partner for justifying the adjustments that are now quietly contemplated. Finally, in the area of conflict resolution, prospects for a timely resolution of the Arab-Israeli conflict remain dim or worse, but the remarkable agreement negotiated under U.S. sponsorship over Northern Ireland is cause for much satisfaction.

Why, then, should Americans seem concerned about the fact and the condition of American leadership and its role in the world—particularly now? A century of increasingly global involvement in the world has left the United States as a power without peer because of the totality of its economic, military, political, and even cultural reach.[14] Alternatives to an effective U.S. leadership are, therefore, few: if not America, then who; if not now, then when? But, it can be asked, why should Americans care about anarchy? Why not retire or, at the very least, rethink the entangling relationships that were developed over the past 50 years in an alleged fit of absent-mindedness?

Again, answers should be all too obvious. America's involvement in the world is not a matter of vocation, but it is not just a matter of position either, although the country has become far too powerful to desist and remain aloof as it once did. Rather, America's involvement in the world is a matter of interests that are much too significant to be viewed as anything less than vital to the nation's welfare and well-being, and far too important to leave them dependent on the will and capabilities of allies, or the intentions and ineptitude of adversaries.

That the world may be wary of American power may well be true, although no ally is showing much interest in being rid of it.[15] That Americans are weary of the world may well be true too. But unlike previous generations, they have become sufficiently aware of the world to be as sensitive to its promises as they are leery of its problems. Forget isolationism and all that: the know-nothings of yesteryear know better now.[16] Calls for restraint in the use of U.S. power are limited to "places where we have no interests" rather than based on a broader sense of national indifference or moral irrelevance.[17] Calls for selective unilateralism are mainly justified by the absence of willing posses of states for specific tasks, rather than in terms of a broad decline that has exposed the irreversible limits of U.S. power. Calls against using that power may well reflect an aversion to pain that contradicts an urge for dominance. In an increasingly civil world in which affluence need not rhyme with dominance and is unquestionably defeated by war, this apparent contradiction needs no apology, assuming it ever did.[18] In short, Americans will do what they believe is needed so long as they are told what it takes and why.

What is lacking after the Cold War is not a new vision of world order. There is a vision, already, stated and tested during the many years of cold war and the many years before. It is a vision based on the "self-evident truths" and "inalienable rights" of the American Republic. That most nations, and all citizens within each nation, can now seek "life, liberty, and the pursuit of happiness" more openly, and achieve these more widely and more safely, than ever before is not the least achievement of the twentieth century. Enlarging the democratic space thus defined is not a modest vision. It can do for now.

What is needed after the Cold War is a will for leadership now, rather than the memories of past leadership. Pessimism about order in the world and doubts about U.S. leadership reflect much ambivalence over the accomplishments that lie behind. By the standards of history no less than by the standards of self-interest, the role the United States played in the world has been extraordinarily effective. Why not tell the American people about it, then—why not speak to them about foreign policies with the same conviction and assertiveness? Internationalism is not shameful, always to be endured but never to be mentioned. Public support for foreign policy is a process of education.[19] People must be told about the problems and risks the nation faces in the world, about proposed solutions and the threats they entail, as well as the greater risks that failure to achieve the desired objectives would entail.

America is not a nation of passive and slightly embarrassed voyeurs. Americans are active and proud doers who have gained the right to be told what their leaders are doing in the world, and why. When in doubt, they will listen to explanations, and they will learn to understand their interests better, as they did when they heard out the president whose role in history, played halfway into the twentieth century, was being remembered 50 years later.

Notes

1. Simon Serfaty, "No More Dissent," *Foreign Policy* no. 11 (Summer 1973): 144–158.

2. G. John Ickenberry, "The Future of International Leadership," *Political Science Quarterly* 111, no. 3 (1996): 386–387.

3. Henry Kissinger, *The White House Years* (Boston, Mass.: Little, Brown, 1979), 49–53.

4. Zbigniew Brzezinski, *Power and Principle* (New York: Farrar, Straus, Giroux, 1983), 81. For example, "Carter Pledges Continuity in Foreign Policy," and "Carter Gets Briefing By Kissinger and Sees a Smooth Transition," *New York Times*, November 5 and 21, 1976, respectively. Carter's influence in the world grew during the presidential transition over a wide range of issues. For example, "Brezhnev Appeals to Carter to Push Stalled Arms Pact," and "Carter Backs Move for European Parley," *New York Times*, December 1, 1976, and January 6, 1977, respectively.

5. "Now Bowing Out, A Busy, Busy Bush," *New York Times*, January 1, 1993, p. A8; "Aides Say U.S. Role in Somalia Gives Bush a Way to Exit in Glory," December 6, 1992, p. A14; "Transatlantic Impasse," November 7, 1992, p. A1; "Trade Pact Signed in Three Capitals," December 18, 1992, p. D1; "Bush's Last Hurrahs in Cold, Wintry Moscow," January 3, 1993, p. A8; "U.S. Sends Flotilla to Prevent Exodus from Haiti by Sea," January 16, 1993, p. A1; "Bush Warns Serbs Not to Widen War," December 28, 1992, p. A6;

"U.S. Hopes to Broaden Ban on Arms Sales to Iran," November 18, 1992, p. A5; "Bush Sends Final Message to His Old Nemesis in Iraq," January 14, 1993, p. A9. So it went to the last three days, November 18–19–20, when front-page headlines on the *New York Times* all emphasized the "U.S.-Led Raids on Iraq."

6. Richard Holbrooke, *To End a War* (New York: Random House, 1998), 66–68.

7. Richard Holbrooke, "America as a European Power," *Foreign Affairs* 74, no. 2 (March/April 1995): 44–45. James M. Goldgeiger, "NATO Expansion: The Anatomy of a Decision," *Washington Quarterly* 21, no. 1 (Winter 1998): 85–102. Jonathan Eyal, "NATO's enlargement: anatomy of a decision," *International Affairs* 73, no. 4 (Autumn 1997).

8. From early 1995 on, Holbrooke, the main architect of enlargement, was explicit about the three candidates he favored. Why the European allies were surprised in the spring 1997, when the U.S. preference became official at last, is itself surprising. One year before the 1997 summit in Madrid, former U.S. ambassador to Poland Donald Blanken was equally explicit, as he wrote "America's Stake in NATO Enlargement," *Wall Street Journal*, July 5, 1996. On both questions, who and when, also see Simon Serfaty, "All in the Family," *Current History* 93, no. 586 (November 1994): 353–358, and "Half Before Europe, Half Past NATO," *Washington Quarterly* 18, no. 2 (March 1995): 49–58.

9. Steven Kull, "Americans on NATO Enlargement," PIPA-4, Program on International Policy Attitudes, Center for International and Security Studies at Maryland (CISSM), February 23, 1998, p. 2. Clinton's reluctance to make the case for enlargement is significant for the impact it may have on the debate that will surround future decisions on NATO. See, for example, Charles Krauthammer, "Good Geopolitics," *Washington Post*, April 17, 1998.

10. Anthony Lake, "Confronting the Backlash States," *Foreign Affairs* 173, no. 2 (March/April 1994); Martin Indyck, "The Clinton Administration's Approach to the Middle East," Washington, D.C.: Washington Institute for Near East Policy, May 18, 1993.

11. For example, in President Clinton's 1998 State of the Union Message, and in his speech at the Pentagon three weeks later, February 17, 1998.

12. George Kennan, *Memoirs* (Boston, Mass.: Little, Brown, 1977), 53.

13. Kissinger, *White House Years*, 18.

14. Joseph S. Nye, Jr., *Bound to Lead: The Changing Nature of American Power* (New York: Basic Books, 1990).

15. The USIA Office of Research and Media Reaction usefully tracks foreign reactions to the United States. For example, "Trend Analysis: Mixed Assessments of U.S. 'Undisputed' Role as Superpower," *Daily Digest*, September 29, 1997. Stan Sloan, "The U.S. Role in the World: Indispensable

Leader or Hegemon?" CRS Report for Congress 9701946 F, December 10, 1997, p. 3.

16. Jeremy D. Rosner, "The Know-Nothings Know Something," *Foreign Policy*, no. 101 (Winter 1995/96): 120.

17. Martin Walker, "The New American Hegemony," *World Policy Journal* 13, no. 2 (Summer 1996): 14. John Hillen, "Superpowers Don't Do Windows," *Orbis* 41, no. 2 (Spring 1997): 241.

18. Robert W. Tucker, "The Future of a Contradiction," *National Interest*, Spring 1996, p. 20.

19. Stanley Hoffmann, *Primacy or World Order: American Foreign Policy Since the Cold War* (New York: McGraw Hill, 1978), 312. Will Friedman and John Immerwahr, "Discussing Foreign Policy with the Post-Cold War Public," *Brown Journal of World Affairs* 3, issue 1 (Winter/Spring 1996): 261.

Index

Agricultural sector. *See* Common Agricultural Policy (CAP), European Union.
Albright, Madeleine, 117
Algeria: current crisis of, 81, 95; economic performance in, 85, 88–89; economic space, 85; Euro-Atlantic policy toward, 97; European concerns with crisis in, 86–92; post-1995 constitutional legitimacy, 95–96; role of Islam in, 82–85
Annan, Kofi, 115
Arab-Israeli conflict: future crisis of, 95
Arab-Israeli peace process: deteriorating, 113, 116; U.S. approach to, 34
Austria: as potential NATO member, 68
Aziz, Tariq, 115

Baker, James, 95
Balkan states: European concerns related to, 40; European reaction to actions of, 131; instability and uncertainty in, 30; wish for NATO membership, 134
Balladur, Edouard, 87
Baltic states: potential for NATO membership, 67; wish for NATO membership, 134
Benjedid, Chadli, 82
Blair, Tony, 26, 35, 54
Bosnia: Clinton's management of, 130–132; effect of perceived failure in, 62; U.S. troop deployment in, 61; war in, 31, 38
Boumediene, Houari, 82
Bulgaria, 58, 134

Bush, George, 127–128, 130, 134
Byrnes, James, 124–125

Central and Eastern European countries (CCEE): applicants for membership, 55–57; chosen for EU membership, 54; expansion of EU to, 47–48; large agricultural sectors of, 55–57
Chernomyrdin, Victor, 49
China, 116
Chirac, Jacques, 5, 26, 36, 47, 87, 111
Clinton, William J.: announcement related U.S. troops in Bosnia (1997), 61; characterization of Saddam and his regime, 135; compared to Harry Truman, 127; development of foreign policy agenda, 129–130; management of Bosnia, 130–132; perceived understanding of the world, 128; weakness in foreign policy arena, 135–136
Clinton administration, 59, 62; potential to impose ILSA on Total company, 114; prediction related to Persian Gulf and Arab-Israeli conflict, 115
Club Med, 93–94
Cold War: Algerian crisis inherited from, 81–92; detente during, 113; effect and legacy of, 17, 72–73; Europe's discoveries during, 6; NATO and EU interdependencies and policies developed during, 52–53, 57; NATO's transformation at end of,

Cold War (*continued*)
    130; United States at end of, 28;
    U.S. leadership during, 57, 127
Common Agricultural Policy (CAP),
    European Union, 23, 48, 55–56
Common Foreign and Security Policy
    (CFSP), 23; conditions for launch
    of, 38–39; developed at IGC
    (1996), 53–54; imperative to fulfill,
    99
Communism, 26, 35
Cook, Robin, 118
Cyprus, 47, 54, 62, 93, 95
Czech Republic, 50

d'Alema, Massimo, 26
Dayton agreements (1995), 40, 61–62
de Charette, Hervé, 114, 117
Dual containment policy, U.S.: assump-
    tions of, 134–135; in the Persian
    Gulf, 113, 117

Economic and Monetary Union (EMU):
    as center of EU attention, 38;
    debate related to, 25; debate related
    to enlargement of, 64
Estonia, 50, 69
Euro, the: introduction of (1999), 5, 25,
    37; long-term potential for, 21–22,
    40, 56, 64–66; predictions related
    to performance of, 65–66, 70; sur-
    render of national currencies to, 57
Euro-American space, 17, 53, 72
Euro-Atlantic security space, 42–43, 53,
    72
Europe: events changing course of histo-
    ry in, 31–32; followership of, 27,
    117; future of, 4–5; future of Cold
    War legacies in Western, 39–43;
    future of U.S. involvement in,
    47–52; as integrated union, 12,
    14–15, 20–21, 32–33; interests in
    Persian Gulf and Greater Middle
    East, 107–111; Left-Right cleavage

in nations of, 26, 32–35; need for
    U.S. and NATO support, 94–95;
    past and legacy of, 12–14; position
    on U.S. Persian Gulf policies, 112;
    post–Cold War instability and
    uncertainty, 30–31; post–Cold War
    political mood, 26; questioning
    U.S. leadership in, 39; question of
    Islam in, 33–34; relations with
    Middle East, 111–114; Russia's
    problems, 63; security challenges
    in, 40–41; southern EU members
    in agricultural policy debate,
    55–56; unhappiness with EU and
    NATO limits, 24–25, 37; United
    States as Great Power in, 43, 57 *See
    also* Western Europe.
European Central Bank (ECB), 22, 38,
    48, 57
European Commission *Agenda 2000*, 25,
    48
European Community (EC): preparation
    for Single Market, 53
European Council: decisions related to
    future EU membership, 47–48;
    probable changes related to
    enlarged membership, 48
European Union (EU): agenda
    (1999–2003), 21–22, 37; benefits
    from membership in WEU, 68;
    budget reform and spending cap,
    55–56; commitment for free trade
    area with North Africa, 94;
    Common Agricultural Policy
    reform, 23, 48, 55–56; Common
    Foreign and Security Policy, 23,
    38–39, 53–54, 99; defining Euro-
    American space, 17–18; economic
    space of, 43, 47–48; effect of cen-
    tral bank development on, 48;
    European nation-states transformed
    into, 15; future of, 5–7; new mem-
    bers, 30; outcome of IGC (1996),
    53–54; post–Cold War enlarge-
    ment and reform, 41–43; proposed
    integration of WEU into, 23; role

of southern-shore Mediterranean countries for, 80; as U.S. interest, 18, 29, 57 *See also* Economic and Monetary Union (EMU); Euro, the.

European Union (EU) enlargement: debate related to membership in, 47–50; differences from NATO enlargement, 50–52; effect of, 66–67; effect of delays to enlarge, 69; moving parallel to NATO enlargement, 57–66

Fini, Gianfranco, 35, 36
Finland, 68
Foreign policy, U.S.: after World War II, 124–126; after World War II in Europe, 29; Clinton's development of his agenda, 129; question of Clinton's leadership of, 135–140; related to terrorism, 116; during transition from Bush administration, 127–129 *See also* Dual containment policy, U.S..
Former Soviet republics: future of, 30; potential for NATO membership, 67
France: concerns with Algerian crisis, 86–92; end of no–fly zone participation in Iraq, 115; interest in North Africa, 92–93; leading Eurofor and Euromarfor forces, 94; Muslims in, 107–108; objections to U.S. policy over UN weapons inspectors, 115; outcome of legislative elections in, 36; political change in (1958–1963), 33; potential populist challenge to Europe, 36; relationship with Britain, 23; relationship with Germany, 22–23
Free trade area (FTA), EU-North Africa, 94
Front de Libération Nationale (FLN), Algeria, 81–82
Front Islamique du Salut (FIS), Algeria, 82–84, 86, 87
Front National, France, 79

Germany: dominance of, 16; immigrants in, 88; Muslims in, 107–108; political change in (1958–1963), 33; relationship with France, 22–23; reunification of, 30; as viewed by Arab world, 107
Great Britain: growing influence of, 118; Labour Party policy toward Europe, 23; relationship with France, 23; as viewed by Arab world, 107
Greece, 58
Groupe Islamique Armé (GIA), Algeria, 83–84, 87
Gulf Cooperation Council (GCC), 115
Gulf War (1991), 127; U.S. strategy after, 113, 115–116
Gulf wars (1980–1988; 1991), 106

Hamas, 84
Hassan (king of Morocco), 91–92
Holbrooke, Richard, 131–133

IGC. *See* InterGovernmental Conference (IGC), European Commission.
Immigrants: from former European empires, 33–34; in Germany and Spain, 88; Muslim nationals in Europe, 89–90
Immigration: French regulations related to, 88
Institutions: complex interdependence during Cold War, 52–53; defining Euro-American space, 17; implications of dual enlargement of NATO and EU, 57–73; issues addressed by IGC (1996), 53–55; revisions in governance under Single European Act (1987), 53
InterGovernmental Conference (IGC), European Commission: issues addressed (1996), 53–54; proposed for 2001, 37, 48–49

Iran: foreign investment in oil fields of, 109–110; as potential market for Europe, 109; potential of opening to, 119; Reagan's policy toward, 134; U.S. containment policy, 117; U.S. dual containment against Iraq and, 117; weapons of mass destruction, 110

Iran and Libya Sanctions Act (ILSA), United States, 114

Iraq: Bush's firmness toward, 134; earmarked products of oil fields in, 109; finding policy to deter, 119; inconclusive military confrontations, 63; issue of lifting UN embargo, 115; as potential market for Europe, 109; Reagan's accommodation of, 134; U.S. dual containment against Iran and, 117; weapons of mass destruction, 110

Ireland, 68, 129

Islam: arc of crises along Mediterranean, 33, 79–80, 105; as destructive force, 110–111; presence in Europe, 34, 107–108; radicalization in Europe of Islamic diaspora, 34; role in Algeria, 82–85; role in independent Algerian state, 81–82

Italy: interests in Maghreb countries, 93; neo-Fascist party, 35; participation in land- and sea-based forces, 94; political change in (1958–1963), 33; as viewed by Arab world, 107

Johnson, Lyndon B., 128
Jospin, Lionel, 26, 35, 36, 54

Kennan, George, 136
Kinkel, Klaus, 111–112
Kissinger, Henry, 128, 136
Kohl, Helmut, 5, 25, 26, 47, 54
Kosovo, 40, 95
Kosygin, Alexei, 128
Kuwait, 116

Latvia, 49

Leadership: European questions about U.S., 27–29; intra-European, 22; in post–Cold War era, 6–7; risks to U. S. of stronger Europe, 57–66; of United States in postwar Europe, 15

Le Pen, Jean-Marie, 87, 90
Libya, 91, 93
Lithuania, 50, 134

Maastricht Treaty (1991): EU enlargement under, 53; political and economic goals under, 59, 99

Major, John, 26

Mediterranean countries: arc of crises in southern shore and along, 33, 79–80, 105; Club Med caucus of EU nations, 93; European-U.S. ties with southern-shore, 97–98; processes of significance for EU and United States, 80

Middle East: arms imports to, 116; Britain's growing influence in, 118; effect on Europe of wars in, 63; European interests in Greater, 106–111; European-U.S. differences related to, 105–106; potential for armed conflict in, 63; potential for instability in, 116; proposed linking of Europe with U.S. initiatives in, 98

Millennium Round, 23
Millon, Charles, 115
Mitterrand, François, 87
Morocco, 91–93
Muslims: potential radicalization of groups, 107–108; settling in Europe, 89–90, 107

NATO: availability of assets to European countries, 94–95; commitment to new members in, 30; debate over post–Cold War future of, 31;

defining Euro-American space, 17, 19; Madrid summit (1997), 68; member commitments at Madrid summit (1997), 68; as tool of United States, 19–20; transformation at end of Cold War, 130

NATO enlargement: beyond nineteen members, 67–68; debate over, 20, 59–61; differences from EU enlargement, 50–52; effect of, 66–67; moving parallel to EU enlargement, 57–66; post–Cold War reform and, 41–43; potential post-1999 new members, 63–64; security context of previous, 34

Nixon, Richard M., 128

North Africa: Algeria as pivot state in, 71–92; EU free trade agreement with, 94; French interest in, 92–100; U.S. interests in, 97

North American Free Trade Agreement (NAFTA), 128

Norway, 49

Organization for Cooperation and Security in Europe (OCSE), 31

Péguy, Charles, 15

Persian Gulf: enforcement of strategy in, 118–120; Euro-American dialogue on, 120; Europe's interests in, 106–111; Europe's position on U.S. policies in, 112–113; future crisis of, 95; proposed reappraisal of dual containment in, 98; U.S. dual containment policy in, 34, 113, 134–135; U.S. failure of will and vision in, 134 *See also* Gulf War.

Poland, 49, 56, 67, 69

Prodi, Romano, 26, 35, 36

Reagan, Ronald, 134

Romania: as potential EU member, 70; as potential member of NATO, 58, 70, 134

Rome Treaties (1957): Britain's refusal to sign, 23; regulations and laws of, 51; vision of EU close union, 64

Russia: arms sales, 116; concern over post–Cold War role, 62; dominance of, 16; expectations for EU membership, 49; impact on NATO and EU of internal issues in, 63; as viewed by Arab world, 107

Saddam Hussein, 112–115, 119, 135

Saudi Arabia, 116

Schengen agreements: demands of, 57; enforcement of, 94

Schroeder, Gerhard, 5, 26, 35

Single European Act (1987), 53

Slovakia, 50

Slovenia, 69, 134

Somalia, 128

Soviet Union, 30, 35, 105

Spain: immigrants in, 88; interests in Morocco and Algeria, 93; participation in land- and sea-based forces, 94; as viewed by Arab world, 107

Sudan, 91

Suez crisis (1956), 106

Sweden, 68

Trade: EU-North Africa free-trade area, 94; Europe-Middle East, 108–109; Iran-Germany (1989–1996), 111

Transatlantic Action Group, proposed, 99

Truman, Harry S., 127

Truman administration, 32, 124–126

Tunisia, 91, 93

Turkey: bid for EU membership, 58, 62; decline in U.S. security assistance to, 62; in first NATO enlargement, 58; potential for crisis in or with, 62

Ukraine, 49

United Arab Emirates, 116

United States: dual containment of Iran and Iraq, 117; encouragement to WEU, 38; Europe's questioning leadership of, 39; future involvement in Europe, 39–44; as Great Power in Europe, 18, 43, 57; interest in EU, 11–12, 18, 29, 57, 72; issue of involvement in Europe, 16–20; leadership after World War II, 15, 124–127; leadership during Cold War, 127; NATO as tool of, 19–20; position at end of Cold War, 28; power accumulated since World War II, 127; proposed role in post–Cold War NATO adaptations, 130; role of southern-shore Mediterranean countries for, 80; security assistance to Turkey, 62;

self-denial, self-deception, and lack of will, 28

Washington Treaty (1949), 30, 51, 61, 92

Weapons of mass destruction (WMDs): European concerns related to Middle East, 110; theater ballistic missiles, 91

Western European Union (WEU): benefits to EU members, 68; future plans for, 38; proposed integration into EU, 23

Yugoslavia, 30

Zeroual, Liamine, 83–88, 96

About the Author

SIMON SERFATY holds a senior professorship in international politics with the Graduate Program in International Studies at Old Dominion University in Norfolk, Virginia, where he teaches graduate seminars in Euro-Atlantic relations and U.S. foreign policy. He also serves as senior associate and director of European Studies at the Center for Strategic and International Studies (CSIS). Previously, he taught at the University of California at Los Angeles (UCLA) and at the Johns Hopkins School of Advanced International Studies (SAIS) in Washington, D.C., where he held the positions of director of the SAIS Center of European Studies in Bologna, Italy (1972–1976), director of the Washington Center of Foreign Policy Research (1978–1980), and executive director of the Johns Hopkins Foreign Policy Institute (1984–1991).

Dr. Serfaty's books include *France, de Gaulle and Europe* (1968), *The Elusive Enemy* (1972), *Fading Partnership* (1979), *The United States, Europe, and the Third World* (1979), *American Foreign Policy in a Hostile World* (1984), *Les années difficiles* (1986), *After Reagan: False Starts, Missed Opportunities, and New Beginnings* (1989), *Taking Europe Seriously* (1992), and *Stay the Course* (1997). Volumes he has edited include *The Future of U.S.-Soviet Relations* (1989), *The Media and Foreign Policy* (1990), and *New Thinking and Old Realities: America, Russia, and Europe* (1991). His essays have appeared in leading professional journals in the United States and in many countries in Europe.

Dr. Serfaty has been a guest lecturer in more than 40 different countries in Europe, Asia, and Africa. He serves on the editorial boards of several journals, including the *Washington Quarterly*, *International Politics*, and *Géopolitique*.